THE CONGRESS OF VIENNA

THE CONGRESS OF VIENNA

1814–1815

SIR CHARLES *Kingsley* WEBSTER

LONDON
THAMES AND HUDSON

The publishers gratefully acknowledge the consent of Lady Webster and the Controller of Her Majesty's Stationery Office to the reissue of this work by the late Sir Charles Webster. Since its first publication by the Foreign Office in 1919, it was reissued in 1934 and reprinted in 1937, 1945 and 1950.

This edition first published in Great Britain 1963
Reprinted 1965

Printed in Great Britain by The Camelot Press Limited,
London and Southampton

21446

CONTENTS

PART ONE

THE PREPARATION OF THE CONGRESS

INTRODUCTION

The late Sir Charles Webster was one of those few British dons who had the opportunity to apply his learning and his meticulously accurate scholarship to the practical problems of policy-making: his talents in this arena were valued highly by the professional diplomats among whom he worked, and the experience which was his gave to his writing and to his teaching a quality which they could not otherwise have had. Born in 1886, he was already a Professor at Liverpool before the First World War, and in subsequent years he held Chairs at Aberystwyth, Harvard and London until his retirement in 1953, eight years before his sudden and unexpected death. The articles and papers which over those years flowed in an almost continuous stream from his pen were backed by several substantial books, of which at least two, *The Foreign Policy of Castlereagh* and *The Foreign Policy of Palmerston*, will stand not only as definitive works of scholarship but as pioneering labours in a field of enquiry not hitherto cultivated by the intensive methods which he employed. In addition to this prolific authorship he spent much time stumping the country in aid of causes in which he believed, particularly on behalf of the League of Nations Union during his years in Wales and after; and his powerful voice which he used to the full, the smacking of his lips, the noisy exhalation of breath, every trick of the practised speaker and some of his own—all these added to the quality and the good sense of what he had to say to make attendance at one of his performances something not easy to forget. His formidable size, his booming voice, his skill in puncturing intellectual pretension or looseness of thought, and his great self-confidence combined to make a somewhat intimidating impression upon students until, when they came to know him better, they found the impression belied by a fund of kindness and an overflowing generosity. In this activity alone was enough for one man's life.

But in intervals formed by the two world wars he was drawn from these academic and proselytising tasks into the centre of policy-making itself. In Hitler's war he was swiftly taken into the Foreign Office, and as the war began to swing towards victory he moved naturally towards the rôle for which his abilities and his training eminently fitted him. At Dumbarton Oaks and again at San Francisco where the Charter of the United Nations was first outlined and then drafted and agreed he was the leading British expert. Of some of his work, particularly his collaboration with Field-Marshal Smuts on the preamble to the Charter, he has already written; but much remains to be said, and some day it will be revealed. At this time all that can be added is that it was for this work that he received his K.C.M.G., an honour which he greatly prized.

But already twenty-seven years earlier, and in a much more junior capacity, he was given what seemed to be an opportunity to contribute to that earlier process of peacemaking, at Paris, after the first great war. In 1917, in preparation for a future peace conference, there was conceived in the Foreign Office the idea of having prepared, under the direction of Alwyn Parker, then Librarian of the Foreign Office, a number of historical studies which might assist the delegates in their negotiations. Webster in the early months of 1918 was a Major in M.I.6 in the War Office, but he badly wanted to share in the work of the peace conference, and early in the spring he was asked by Parker to write a monograph on the Congress of Vienna. The idea of the invitation was suggested to Parker, probably at Webster's instigation, by Charles Orde, a friend of Webster's in the Foreign Office. Parker, though at first sceptical was persuaded by Webster that such a monograph would be valuable.

To carry out the task Webster was seconded for some eleven weeks from the War Office to the Foreign Office, and in that remarkably short period he wrote the masterly little work which is now being reprinted. However much he proclaims in his Preface his avoidance of 'any reference to or comparison with present circumstances, such applications being outside the province of the historian as such', it is certain that he hoped his description of how the Congress of Vienna was managed or mismanaged would save the statesmen of 1919 from many similar errors. In addition to the monograph, he drafted a memorandum (printed for the first time in the 1934 edition of this work), making suggestions about the approaching peace conference for the use of the British delegation. His youthful optimism (an endearing characteristic which remained with him into old age) was to be undeceived. As he notes himself, his work had, so far as he was able to discover, no effect on the statesmen at the conference, or on the conference itself except in some minor details of procedure.

Great or little as was its practical influence, however, as a work of scholarship it retains all its value. The majority of the other monographs written under the auspices of the Foreign Office were intended to provide the British delegates with the information necessary for wise solution of the many problems pressing upon the attention of the conference, problems territorial, constitutional, ethnic, economic and political. Not so Webster's. His prime concern was with the procedures and mechanisms by which these problems were to be discussed and settled. It was a concern which stayed with him throughout his life, believing as he wrote in a Foreword to F. S. Marston's *The Peace Conference of 1919*, which he largely inspired, that 'the methods by which we try to attain our ends are second in importance only to the ends themselves'. The truth of this statement is generally recognised now, particularly after experience of the skill with which Soviet negotiators have used procedural devices to advance their purposes, but it was not so widely seen by scholars or statesmen in 1919.

This book, then, essentially is about the organisation of the Congress of Vienna, the methods and procedures by which decisions were reached, rather than about the decisions themselves. In the hands of many writers such a subject would be dull. Webster, however, succeeds in infusing a sense of high drama into his narrative by his skilful interweaving of the technicalities of his subject with the interplay of personal rivalries and manœuvrings, and the conveyed awareness of the magnitude of the issues involved. The whole is written in a pellucid style foreshadowing the achievement which was to be consummated a dozen or so years later in the *Castlereagh*.

Decision-making analysis is now recognised as providing one possible conceptual framework within which the study of international relations as an academic discipline may be organised. The refinements of thought in this field, the insights and the taxonomy which are now being evolved were not and could not be conceived in 1918, for the relations between states themselves had only recently begun to become more than relations between diplomats, dynasties and professional military. But while there is in Webster no attempt at generalisation or hypothesis of the kind that is currently fashionable, his book is full of illustrative material for generalisation, and it thus has relevance for the contemporary student of international relations as well as being a historical monograph which is not likely to be superseded.

To be able to write these lines as an introduction to this reprinting is to offer a small requital on behalf of so many for the intellectual and personal debt which they owe to one of the great creative historians of this century.

P. A. REYNOLDS

Aberystwyth, July 1962

PREFACE

This monograph was written at the request of the Librarian of the Foreign Office in eleven weeks of this year, extending from May to August. It is purely a *pièce de circonstance*, and will be followed, I hope, by a larger work on the same subject when I am released from my present duties. No one could be more conscious of its faults and omissions than its author; and the only justification for its publication is the fact that it may be of some interest to the general public in view of recent events and present conditions.

It is a surprising but none the less authentic fact that there is no standard history of the Congress of Vienna. We thus stand on the threshold of a new Congress without any adequate account of the only assembly which can furnish even a shadowy precedent for the great task that lies before the statesmen and peoples of the world. This small book makes no pretensions to fill that gap, but it may serve to show how much still remains to be done before the history of the Congress of Vienna is fully known.

I have written for the information of officials and men of action rather than historians, but I have tried to give them some authorities for my conclusions. Throughout I have avoided any reference to or comparison with present circumstances, such applications being outside the province of the historian as such. So far, indeed, as any precedents are provided by this period of history, they may probably be considered useful rather as warnings than as examples; and the book will have served its purpose if it draws attention to some errors of statesmanship, which we may hope will be avoided at the present day.

Fortunately for Englishmen, though no complete work yet

exists on this subject, the brilliant monographs of Professor Alison Phillips in the Cambridge Modern History, as well as his lectures published in the 'Confederation of Europe', have already established Castlereagh's position as a diplomatist; while Sir Adolphus Ward's chapters on the 'Congress of Vienna', also published in the Cambridge Modern History, are the most impartial and authentic account that at present exists of the Congress itself.

The acknowledgements, which I owe to a large number of foreign historians and archivists, I must reserve till the publication of my larger study. I cannot forbear, however, from paying here a tribute to the scholarship and learning of Professor August Fournier, which he placed unreservedly at my disposal; and, like all students of the modern papers at the Record Office, I have experienced the great kindness and patience of Mr. Hubert Hall and Mr. Headlam.

Nor could this little work, produced at such short notice at a time of great pressure, have ever seen the light at all, had it not been for the help and encouragement of friends in London. To Mr. Alwyn Parker, the Librarian of the Foreign Office, who suggested my writing this work; to Dr. G. W. Prothero, the Director of the Historical Section of the Foreign Office, who brought into some shape and form my hastily constructed pages; and to Mr. Moreton Macdonald, Captain C. R. M. Cruttwell, and Dr. Headlam-Morley, who gave me much valuable advice at a time when they were overwhelmed with other important duties, I owe my most grateful thanks, as well as to Major H. W. V. Temperley, who, at considerable inconvenience to himself, procured me an interval in which to write.

The Bibliography merely gives a selection of a few useful authorities. The documents in the Appendix have been read with the original texts, and should prove to be accurate.

CHARLES K. WEBSTER

London, December 1918

PREFACE TO THE SECOND EDITION

This little book has long been out of print and secondhand copies have been sold for absurd prices. Parts of its subject have been more fully dealt with in subsequent publications, but the analysis of the machinery of the Congress has not yet been superseded by a more comprehensive work. I am therefore grateful to H.M. Stationery Office for permission to reprint it. For technical reasons I am unable to make any alterations in the text except of one or two misprints.

I have included, however, by permission of the Foreign Office, my own suggestions made in August 1918 for the approaching Peace Conference which were circulated in a confidential edition to the Members of the British Delegation. I cannot say that they produced much effect except on the waste-paper baskets and one or two other minor problems of organisation. The situation changed a good deal before the Conference met, and those who directed it had little leisure to meditate on historical precedents. Indeed, when on January 28, 1919, one Delegate referred to the Congress of Vienna, President Wilson is recorded to have replied that: 'The present enterprise was very different from that undertaken at Vienna a century ago, and he hoped that even by reference no odour of Vienna would again be brought into their proceedings.' Nor so far as I know was any introduced—by reference.

C. K. W.

August 1934

CHRONOLOGICAL TABLE

1813

February 28   Treaty of Kalisch between Russia and Prussia. (An offensive and defensive alliance against France, which included a secret Russian guarantee for the restoration to Prussia of the political position of 1805.)

March 16   Prussia declares war against France.

June 4   Napoleon concludes the Armistice of Pleswitz with Russia and Prussia.

June 27   Austria concludes the Treaty of Reichenbach with Russia and Prussia, and undertakes to enter the war if Napoleon refuses the terms offered by the Allies.

August 12   Austria declares war on France.

September 9   Treaty of Toeplitz between Austria, Russia, and Prussia.

October 8   Treaty of Ried between Austria and Bavaria.

October 16–19   Battle of Leipzig, after which all Central Europe joins the Allies.

November 9   The 'Frankfurt Proposals', offering France the Rhine boundary.

November 16   Napoleon returns an evasive answer. (Caulaincourt's attempt to revive the proposals is rejected by the Allies in the beginning of December.)

December 26   Castlereagh's Cabinet Memorandum on the British policy towards the Allies and Napoleon.

1814

January 11   Treaty of Alliance between Austria and Naples (Murat).

January 18   Castlereagh arrives at Bâle.

January 29   The 'Langres Protocol', in which the four Allied Powers formulate their peace proposals.

February 5 to March 19		The abortive Conference of Châtillon between the representatives of the Allies and Caulaincourt.
March	9	Treaty of Chaumont (dated March 1) between the four Allied Powers—the 'Quadruple Alliance'.
March	31	The Allies enter Paris. Provisional Government under Talleyrand set up.
April	11	Treaty of Fontainbleau: Abdication of Napoleon.
April	23	Armistice between France and the Allies signed.
May	3	Louis XVIII enters Paris.
May	30	First Peace of Paris.
June and July		The Allied Sovereigns and Ministers visit England.
September	15	Informal Conferences begin at Vienna between the Ministers of the 'Four'.
September	22	Protocol of the 'Four', keeping affairs in their own hands.
September	23	Arrival of Talleyrand.
October to November		Refusal of France and Spain to accept the propositions of the 'Four'. Discussions of the Polish Question. Failure to reach agreement.
October	14	Meeting of the German Powers (Austria, Prussia Bavaria, Hanover, Württemberg) to discuss the German settlement.
November	1	Verification of the full-powers of the Plenipotentiaries begins.
November to December		Deadlock on the Polish-Saxon Question.
December 24		Peace concluded between Great Britain and U.S.A.

1815

January	3	Secret Treaty between the British, Austrian, and French Plenipotentiaries at Vienna.
January	9	France admitted to the Directing Committee.
January	12	First meeting of the Committee of Five.
January to February		Adjustment of the German and Polish territorial problems.
February	3	Wellington arrives at Vienna.
February	15	Castlereagh leaves Vienna. Wellington first English Plenipotentiary.

B

March	1	Napoleon lands in France. The Hundred Days begin.
March	13	The Allies declare Napoleon a public enemy.
March	25	Renewal of the Treaty of Chaumont.
March	28	Wellington leaves Vienna. Clancarty first English Plenipotentiary.
April	11	Austria declares war on Murat.
June	9	Final Act of the Congress of Vienna.
June	18	Waterloo.
September	26	The Treaty of the 'Holy Alliance' between Prussia, Russia, and Austria.
November	20	The second Peace of Paris. Allied troops to occupy the northern provinces. Renewal of the Quadruple Alliance.

THE CONGRESS OF VIENNA
1814–15

Section 1. Introductory

A general account of the formation of the last alliance against Napoleon and of the organisation of the Congress of Vienna has been given in two other papers of this series.[1] The object of the present paper is to describe in some detail the course of the negotiations in the years 1814 and 1815, and especially to show the motives which determined the policy of British statesmen during the period and the methods by which they tried to obtain their ends. During these years, by a series of treaties concluded at Paris and Vienna, the frontiers of almost every country in Europe were to be redrawn, and the overseas possessions of the Continental Powers were to be reallotted on a new basis. The military despotism of Napoleon had completely transformed Europe while the French, Dutch, and Danish colonies had been conquered by Great Britain. The destruction of the Napoleonic Empire, therefore, necessitated both the construction of a new Europe and a new distribution of colonial power; the parallel between the problems of that age and those of the present day is in some respects an exceedingly close one. The Congress met in the autumn of 1814; but it was the result of diplomatic transactions of the earlier part of that year at Paris and elsewhere, and its work was completed by the second Peace of Paris, which was made after the return and second defeat of Napoleon. An attempt

---

[1] *Coalitions, Alliances, and Ententes of more than two Powers since 1729* (No. 158) and *International Congresses* (No. 154) in the Series of 'Peace Handbooks' prepared by the Historical Section of the Foreign Office in which the present work was No. 153.

has been made, therefore, to review events from the entrance of Lord Castlereagh into the council of the Allies in January 1814 until the final conclusion of peace in November 1815.

Though an authoritative history of the Congress of Vienna is still to seek, the plans and motives of the Continental Powers have been studied by many historians, and it appears probable that almost all the available evidence of importance has been published. Less attention has, however, been paid to the policy of Great Britain, and there is still much unpublished material in the Foreign Office papers. This material, as well as some from other archives, has been used in the preparation of the present work.

Part One

THE PREPARATION OF THE CONGRESS

*Section 2. Situation of Europe at the End of the Year 1813.
Policy of the Continental Powers*

By the end of 1813 all Europe north of the Alps was in arms
against Napoleon; and, though French troops still held out in
many of the great fortresses of Central Europe, the armies of
Blücher and Schwarzenberg had crossed the Rhine. This coalition was something very different from all previous combinations against Napoleon. It was a coalition of peoples as well as
Governments. The national movement, which had caused
the failure of Napoleon in Spain and Russia, had also arisen
in Germany, and the great empire of Napoleon, which had
stretched from the Douro to the Niemen, had been dissolved in
the course of a single year. After Napoleon's disastrous failure
in Russia in 1812, Prussia, and then Austria, had joined forces
against him; and, as his power declined, all the minor States
of Germany had, more or less willingly, gone over to the
Coalition. Sweden, Holland, and Portugal were also members,
while in Italy Murat was about to conclude an alliance with
Austria against his brother-in-law. Spain had been liberated,
and Wellington had already entered France in the south. Nothing could save Napoleon from complete defeat if the
Coalition against him held together.

But it was doubtful, to say the least, if the Allies would
remain united. Having driven Napoleon from Central
Europe, they were in no sort of agreement as to how they

would deal with the problems raised by his defeat. The three principal Continental Powers had already made it clear that their interests conflicted as to the division of the spoils. Their political dissensions had been made more serious by personal friction, while their generals were no more in agreement than their statesmen. They had not yet even decided whether their ultimate object was to capture Paris and overthrow Napoleon completely, or merely to compel him to accept a peace which might still leave him the master of a France possessing its 'natural' boundaries of the Pyrenees, the Rhine, and the Alps.

The three great Continental Powers were all autocratic monarchies, and their policy was in each case decided mainly by one man. Alexander I, the Tsar of Russia, personally directed the affairs of his country. After the defeat of Napoleon in Russia, he had engaged his people in the war of liberation much against their wish; but from the first he set himself the task, not only of freeing Europe from the domination of Napoleon, but of leading his armies into Napoleon's capital. The great successes of 1813, culminating in the overwhelming victory of Leipzig, had strengthened this resolve; and the Tsar had already begun to be influenced by the religious emotions which were greatly intensified in the course of this period. The extraordinary vanity of Alexander, as well as his persistence, may be partly explained by his belief that he was the instrument of God. But he was also a man of great intelligence and imagination, with a keen eye for the interests of his country. He had learnt from close intercourse with a number of gifted individuals much about the new forces of nationality and democracy which the French Revolution had liberated, and of which Napoleon had been in succession the instrument, the master, and the victim. Alone of all the statesmen of the Great Alliance he appreciated their strength and possibilities, and to a certain extent he sincerely believed in them and wished to give them expression. But he was never prepared to sacrifice to them his desire to increase his personal reputation or what he conceived to be the interests of his country.

Besides the dethronement of Napoleon, the Tsar had one main object in view. He was now in possession of the Duchy of Warsaw, which Napoleon had created out of the Prussian and most of the Austrian share of the Polish partitions of the eighteenth century. It was his fixed resolve to create from this conquest (to which might possibly be added some parts of the Russian share of the partitions) a united, autonomous, but not independent, kingdom of Poland, over which the Tsar of Russia was to rule. In this design he was supported by the Polish nobility, whom the defeat of Napoleon had left to the mercy of their former conquerors; and the pose of generosity towards them was as precious to him as the increase of territory which the plan would give to his dominions. His Russian subjects were as much opposed to this plan, at any rate to the political aspect of it, as they had been to the prosecution of the European war. But his Ministers now and throughout the period were nearly all of non-Russian blood. Stein, the German patriot; Czartoryski, the most influential of Polish nobles; Capo d'Istria, a native of Corfu; together with Laharpe, the Swiss republican, were the men to whom he turned for advice on affairs of State. Anstett, an Alsatian with Polish possessions, who had long been in the Russian diplomatic service, was often used for delicate negotiations. Nesselrode, the Foreign Secretary, also of German blood, was just beginning to be known. His ideas were very different from those of his master, but his influence was small. He was a secretary, and not a Minister. His real importance soon came to lie in the fact that he became a medium through which Metternich and Castlereagh attempted to thwart the wishes of the Tsar. They supplied him with facts and arguments, with which he endeavoured, at this period more often than not in vain, to influence the policy of his master.

Next to Alexander, Metternich had been the principal figure of the Alliance in 1813. In a sense, he had controlled its decisions more than any other single man. The doubtful issue of the first conflicts between Napoleon and the Russo-Prussian forces had given him a position as mediator of which he had made skilful use, and he maintained in some sense this rôle to the end of the year.

As the complete defeat of Napoleon was seen to be more and more probable, Metternich had become increasingly alarmed at the plans of Alexander, and sought already for some combination to keep him in check.

A timid statesman, though fertile in diplomatic expedients, he was an opportunist pure and simple.

The designs of Russia on Poland, as well as those of Prussia on Saxony, he was determined to frustrate if he could; but he regarded the first as by far the more dangerous of the two. Though he did not yet see his way clear, his policy was to awake every possible suspicion against Alexander, and gradually to build up an alliance against him. For this purpose he was using every expedient to detach Prussia and other German States from Russian influence. The dynastic connection between the Habsburgs and Napoleon provided him with another weapon which he was prepared to use if necessary; while, more than any other Continental statesman, he realised the strength of Great Britain, and the possibility that her influence would determine the character of the settlement. Metternich was in almost complete control of Austrian policy. Schwarzenberg, the nominal generalissimo of the alliance, for the most part agreed with him at this time; but an opposition group was forming which looked to Stadion, a former Chancellor, but now subordinate to Metternich, to lead them. The Emperor, Francis I, however, a colourless, though occasionally obstinate man, was, on the whole, under his influence, and Metternich was generally at liberty to act as he thought fit.

Prussian policy was directed by the Chancellor, Hardenberg; but, partly owing to his physical infirmities, he never obtained such an ascendancy as that of Metternich. Humboldt, who acted as his second, had necessarily to transact much business, and his influence greatly increased in the course of the year. The weak and sensitive King of Prussia, Frederick William III, was devoted to Alexander; while the Prussian generals, especially Gneisenau, had views and objects of their own. Hardenberg came under the influence of Metternich, and later of Castlereagh; and, if his position was much stronger than that of Nesselrode, he was used to a certain extent in the same way. Still, he had a considerable power of transacting business, and was one of the principal figures of the Great Alliance. Like all Prussians, he expressed always, and without abatement, an undying hatred of France, which no victories or conquests could assuage.

Of the minor Powers, Sweden was now ruled by the French Marshal Bernadotte, who obtained notoriety by his designs on the French throne, which were supported by Alexander. Denmark had suffered like Saxony, though not in the same degree, for her support of Napoleon. Hanover was represented by Count Münster, who was the trusted confidant, not only of the Prince Regent of England, but also of Castlereagh. But, though a skilled and shrewd observer, he did not contribute very much to decisions except those affecting the interior politics of Germany. Bavaria, who changed sides in the nick of time, Baden, and Württemberg hoped to gain as much from the destruction of French power in Germany as they had obtained by their subservience to Napoleon. Holland was controlled by British policy. Spain, with her colonies in open revolt, and impotent outside the Peninsula, was too proud to admit her weakness, and hoped to re-establish her influence in Italy. Portugal, whose Court was in Brazil, depended, like Holland, on Great Britain. Sardinia-Piedmont had a policy of its own; but Sicily was, at this date, controlled by Great Britain. The minor States, both of Germany and Italy, were, in fact, pawns at the disposition of the Great Powers. The Pope had only just recovered his personal liberty, and had lost practically all influence. The Sultan also had been, to a great extent, outside the orbit of European affairs since the Peace of Bucarest (1812) with Russia. All the minor States knew that the Great Powers could do what they liked with the Napoleonic Empire if only they remained united.

But, as has already been indicated, the Great Powers were far from being united. Their rivalry and suspicion increased as it became clear that the Napoleonic Empire was completely dissolved. The various treaties concluded in the course of the year 1813 had been made purposely vague, except on a few points, and provided neither a specific object to pursue nor machinery by which to pursue it. Thus by the Treaty of Kalisch of February 28, 1813, concluded after much hesitation on the part of Frederick William, Russia had guaranteed by a secret article to restore Prussia to the political and financial position she occupied prior to 1806. The restoration of Polish territory necessary to join Silesia to Old Prussia was specifically mentioned, but, apart from this, it was clear that Russia intended to retain all Prussian Poland. The Treaty of Reichenbach, however, concluded between Austria, Russia, and Prussia during the armistice of Pleswitz, and signed on June 27, 1813, immediately after Napoleon had rejected Austria's mediation, had laid down that the fate of the Duchy of Warsaw should be decided by the three Powers in concert, without the concurrence of France. These two treaties were reinforced by the Treaties of Toeplitz, concluded on September 9, 1813, by which Russia agreed with Austria and Prussia that their States should be reconstructed on the scale of their possessions in 1805, while the Confederation of the Rhine and all Napoleon's other creations beyond the Rhine or the Alps were to be dissolved, Hanover was to be restored, an amicable arrangement was to be made as to the Duchy of Warsaw, and Austria was to recover her provinces on the Adriatic. Thus but little had been definitely settled as to the disposal of Napoleon's Empire, except that Prussia and Austria were to be at least as big as in 1805. Other treaties which were concluded with the minor Powers, such as the Treaty of Ried, between Bavaria and Austria (October 8, 1813), by which the latter Power obtained the promise of Tirol, had not been accepted by all the members of the Alliance, since it was impossible to decide the fate of the conquered territories while the claims of the Great Powers themselves were still unsatisfied. Sweden, who had received the promise of Norway from Russia in 1812 (subsequently confirmed by Great Britain in a subsidy treaty of 1813), was in a sense the only Power which had been granted a specific extension of territory that satisfied its expectations. Nearly all the rest of the reconstruction of Europe was still a matter of dispute.

After Leipzig the aims of the Treaties of Toeplitz seemed to have been attained; and Metternich persuaded both the Tsar and Lord Aberdeen—then the British representative accredited to the Austrian Court—that an answer should be made to Napoleon's recent offer of negotiations. This was done on November 7, through the intermediary of St. Aignan, whom Metternich informed, in the presence of Nesselrode and Aberdeen, that the French territories must be reduced to the 'natural limits' of the Rhine, the Alps, and the Pyrenees. An offer based on these terms was sent to Napoleon on November 9. This offer, which is known as the 'Frankfurt proposals', was made with the concurrence of Alexander as well as of Aberdeen; and the latter had even promised to restore some of the

French colonies, and neglected to make any effective protest against the British maritime law being brought into the discussion. How far the offer was sincerely meant has been doubted by some historians;[1] but, in view of the grave dissensions between the Continental Powers, it is probable that Napoleon could have had peace on these terms had he accepted the offer at once; and Great Britain, committed to a certain extent through Aberdeen's imprudence, would have been powerless to prevent it, however much she might have objected. But Napoleon already saw opposition rising to his power in France, and he could not accept such terms except at the risk of his throne. He still hoped to better his position, and therefore returned an evasive answer (November 16); and, when a fortnight later Caulaincourt, his new Foreign Minister, declared himself ready to accept the terms, it was then too late. The Allied armies were in march towards the Rhine, and the opportunity was lost. Before he could again enter into negotiation Castlereagh was at Allied Headquarters.

Section 3. *The Policy of the British Government. The Character and Aims of Castlereagh*

Throughout the year the British Government had acted as the paymaster of the Coalition, and had endeavoured to combine all Europe towards the common end. But it had exercised little influence on the diplomatic transactions between the Powers or on their negotiations with Napoleon. Its representatives on the Continent with the Great Powers were not men of sufficient weight to obtain a commanding influence, and only imperfectly understood the problems with which they had to deal. Of these, Viscount Cathcart and Sir Charles

[1] Sorel, *L'Europe et la Révolution française*, VIII, 200; but see Fournier, *Napoleon I*, Eng. edn., II, 330. The other British representatives, including Stewart, were furious with Aberdeen. *Diaries and Letters of Sir George Jackson*, II, 360, 368, 376.

Stewart (Castlereagh's half-brother), attached to the Russian and Prussian headquarters respectively, were soldiers rather than diplomatists. The Earl of Aberdeen, sent out in August as Ambassador to Austria, then a young man, was not subtle enough to cope with Metternich, though not so simple as the Austrian diplomatists thought him. He had certainly not played the part expected of him at the time of the Frankfurt proposals. These ambassadors had been specially instructed to make an offensive and defensive alliance with the European Powers, but their personal jealousies and the rivalries of the Powers to which they were accredited made it impossible for them to do so. The treaties between the Continental Powers were drawn up and generally signed before the British representatives were informed; while the British treaties were almost entirely confined to subsidies and the conduct of the war. Only the reconstruction of Hanover, a point which affected the Royal Family, had been promised to Great Britain. Her interests in Spain, Sicily, and, most important of all, in Belgium had not been considered; and how far she was from obtaining security for the last was seen in the Frankfurt proposals, which would have left Antwerp in French hands.

Thus at the end of 1813 the Alliance appeared to be dissolving into fragments. It had neither military nor diplomatic unity. It had neither decided to overthrow Napoleon nor devised any method either of obtaining peace or of prosecuting war. The task of reconciling the differences of the Allies, of binding them closer together, of creating machinery by which they could act in unison against Napoleon, and of providing some plan by which Europe could be reorganised so as to obtain a period of stability after a generation of warfare, was largely the work of Great Britain, and more especially of her Minister for Foreign Affairs, Lord Castlereagh.

The character and achievements of Castlereagh, Foreign Minister since 1812, were long misunderstood, owing to party prejudice and the lack of scientific research. More recently justice has been done to his career by historians, as the Foreign Office papers have been more closely studied; and, if the favourable estimate which Lord Salisbury formed in 1861 has not been entirely confirmed, yet it has been clearly proved that for courage and common sense he has rarely been equalled among British diplomatists, and that his influence over the settlement of 1814-15 was greater than that of any other European statesman. By working with intense energy, and utilising to the full his unique opportunities, he acquired a great knowledge of Continental affairs, and became one of the least insular of British Foreign Ministers. Brought up amidst the passions roused by the conflict with the French Revolution and Napoleon, his dominating idea was naturally security against France, to obtain which he had in his mind various schemes, partly inherited from Pitt, partly devised by himself to suit the exigencies of the time. He was now to endeavour to bring these into operation with a large measure of success; and it will be seen that in the negotiations of these years it was on many occasions Castlereagh who provided the plan of action and eventually secured its acceptance by the Allies.

By obtaining at the earliest possible opportunity the recognition in treaties by the other Powers of the special interests of Great Britain, he was left free to act throughout 1814 and 1815 as mediator in the disputes between his Allies. He suffered some grave defeats, but on the whole the main outlines of his policy are clearly apparent in the treaties which governed Europe for over thirty years. This work he did almost entirely in the council chamber. He was no orator, though he could marshal facts clearly, and he never had any hold on the imagination of his contemporaries. He knew how to manage the House of Commons; but, associated as he was with and approving, as he did, of a reactionary domestic policy, he was hated and despised by the growing liberal forces in England.

He failed, as almost all his contemporaries failed, to see the strength of the national and democratic forces which the French Revolution had liberated. He had not that sympathy with liberal and national ideas which Canning acquired and used later to the great advantage of England and Europe. But within his limits he was clear-sighted and courageous, a real statesman in that his policy was founded on principle, a real diplomatist in that he was fertile in expedients to put his principles into action.

Throughout his career he found little support in his Cabinet. The Tory Ministry of Liverpool contained few men of much intelligence; and they knew little, and cared less, about the affairs of Europe. The Earl of Liverpool had, indeed, to concern himself closely with foreign policy, which the English Prime Minister must always, in a sense, direct and formulate in the Cabinet. But he was a man of only moderate parts; and, while nearly always loyal to Castlereagh, he had little real sympathy with anything which did not concern a purely British interest. It was only the Foreign Minister who saw that the interests of Great Britain were bound up with those of Europe. Wellington, owing to his intercourse with Continental statesmen, came to share and support this view; but the only other prominent Minister ever associated with Castlereagh who had a knowledge of Europe was Canning, who had no influence on events at this time. The Prince Regent himself, who had a shrewd knowledge of men and affairs, was also conversant with European politics. But he was influenced largely by personal motives, was not to be depended upon in a crisis, and, owing to his own unpopularity, was not in a position to give much assistance. His vanity, moreover, often made him interfere in affairs in a most inopportune manner; and his co-operation was often more embarrassing than helpful, and in many cases intended to secure objects which Castlereagh had no wish to obtain.

The British Cabinet had already been informed by their representatives of the growing disunion amongst the Allies. The discussions of Frankfurt, with their references to British maritime rights and surrender of colonies, and the absence of any guarantee of her special interests, showed how little England could expect unless she were better represented in the councils of the Alliance. Castlereagh was in sympathy with the growing desire in Great Britain that Napoleon should be dethroned, and already hoped for a peace which would confine France within her 'ancient limits'. He was determined, above all, that Antwerp should not be left in French hands; and this was the main point that he pressed on Aberdeen in the autumn of 1813.[1] But the problems were so difficult and pressing that it was decided that Castlereagh himself must proceed to the Continent. His representatives were not in agreement amongst themselves, and it was impossible to ascertain from them clearly the policy of the different Courts to which they were accredited. Some special effort was necessary to weld more closely together the Alliance, in which the elements of disruption were already to be clearly discerned, and to endeavour to make it the instrument of British policy on the Continent of Europe. Thus, at the end of December, Castlereagh set out for the Allied Headquarters, taking with him Robinson, the Vice-President of the Board of Trade, as his assistant. His instructions, contained in the form of a Cabinet Memorandum written in his own hand, were dated December 26, 1813. They contain the policy which he was, on the whole, to carry out to a successful conclusion during the next two years.

---

[1] Castlereagh to Aberdeen, Nov. 13, 1813, *Castlereagh Correspondence*, IX, 75;—'The destruction of that arsenal is essential to our safety. To leave it in the hands of France is little short of imposing upon Great Britain the charge of a perpetual war establishment.'

Section 4. The Memorandum of December 26, 1813, on the Negotiations for Peace

The instructions[1] were written from inadequate information as to the intentions of the Allies. They had to provide for various contingencies which depended on the military situation and the persistence of the Powers in pursuing their ends. They were naturally dictated mainly by purely British interests, but these were brought into relation to the general scheme of reconstruction of the Continent, and it was clearly recognised that the one depended on the other.[2] Before the instructions were drawn up, and before it had even been decided to allow Castlereagh to go to the Continent, the Ambassadors of Austria, Prussia, and Russia had been induced to agree that the question of British maritime rights should not even be discussed during the negotiations, Aberdeen's negligence at Frankfurt thus being repaired. But this fundamental condition of the peace negotiations was to be again secured from the Allied Ministers themselves at headquarters immediately on Castlereagh's arrival. The British doctrines on this subject, which had been so often challenged by France, with the sympathy of many other nations, and for which England was even then at war with the United States, were to be accepted in full, both by the Allies and France, as the law of nations without further question before any negotiations with the enemy could be begun.

When he had fully secured this point, Castlereagh was

'to establish a clear and definite understanding with the Allies, not only on all matters of common interest, but upon such

---

[1] F.O. Continent Archives, I. See an article by Mr. G. W. T. Omond in the *Nineteenth Century*, Mar. 1918.
[2] Castlereagh had discussed the whole question with Prince Lieven, the Russian Ambassador, and Pozzo di Borgo, who had been sent over by Alexander specially for the purpose.—Jartens, F., *Recueil des Traités conclus par la Russie*, XI, 198.

C

points as are likely to be discussed with the enemy, so that the several Allied Powers may in their negotiations with France act in perfect concert, and together maintain one common interest'.

For this 'common interest' Great Britain was prepared to cede a large portion of the French and Dutch and Danish colonies which she held. If, however, a peace were made which failed to obtain the cardinal points of British policy, these conquests were to be retained as a security against French Power. The objects which were made specific conditions of the restoration of the British conquests were: (1) The absolute exclusion of France from any naval establishment on the Scheldt, and especially at Antwerp. (2) The establishment of the security of Holland by giving to that Power a barrier in the Netherlands which should include Antwerp. (3) The complete freedom of Spain and Portugal, and the guarantee of their European territory by the Continental Powers against attack from France. Under these conditions Great Britain was prepared to consider as 'objects of negotiation' all her conquests from France except Malta, the Mauritius and Bourbon Isles, and the Saintes Islands, as also Guadeloupe, which had already been promised to Sweden in 1813. This last, however, might possibly be given to France, and Sweden compensated.

The fate of the whole of the Netherlands, however, could not yet be definitely settled, since the extent to which the whole could be wrested from France was yet uncertain. If Austria wished to resume her old possession she was to be supported, but this was not expected. The really essential port was Antwerp and the barrier round it, which was held to be as essential to the security of the Continent as to that of Great Britain. Only if this point was secured were the colonial conquests to be surrendered. The instructions were explicit on this question:

'As the barrier for Holland is an object most deeply interesting to all the Allies, Great Britain is willing to purchase it by a double sacrifice, by cessions both to France and to Holland. If the Allies should not carry this point, so important to their own security, as well as to that of Great Britain, the latter Power will, in that case, have no other alternative than to preserve her colonial conquests as a counterfoil to the dominion of the enemy, and on these grounds to withold these cessions, which she would otherwise be prepared to make to France. The cession of the conquests by Great Britain being declared to be contingent upon equivalent securities to result from the Continental arrangements, and especially on the side of Holland and the Low Countries, any general stipulation which does not expressly declare the principle by which it is to be regulated, and connect it pointedly with these objects appears objectionable.'

It was also the intention of the British Government to obtain a dynastic connection with Holland by a marriage between Princess Charlotte of Wales and the Prince of Orange. For this Castlereagh was first to obtain the assent of the Prince himself, and then open the matter confidentially with the allied sovereigns at headquarters.

Other matters were indicated as desirable, but not made conditions *sine quibus non*. Thus the restoration of the ancient States of Italy was recommended as 'highly expedient', especially that of the King of Sardinia, who, it was suggested, should receive Genoa. British mediation was offered to help to settle internal German affairs. She was also to declare herself ready to sign a peace with the United States 'without involving in such treaty any decision upon the points in dispute at the commencement of hostilities'. Subsidies were to be granted to the Continental Powers; but here again opportunity was to be taken to insist on 'the signing of such engagements, especially as to Holland and the Peninsula, as may justify so great an exertion on the part of Great Britain'.

Lastly, a point of great importance, the alliance against

France was to continue after peace had been made. The construction of a defensive and offensive alliance had been vainly pressed on the Powers in the autumn of 1813. It was now intended to make an alliance whose objects should not be limited to the present emergency.

> 'The Treaty of Alliance,' ran the instructions, 'is not to terminate with the war, but to contain defensive engagements, with mutual obligations to support the Powers attacked by France, with a certain extent of stipulated succours. The *casus fœderis* is to be an attack by France on the European dominions of any one of the contracting parties.'

Both Spain and Holland were to be included in the Alliance, as well as the Great Powers, but it was the latter whom it was especially meant to bind. This project was the origin of the Quadruple Alliance created at Chaumont by Castlereagh as a special safeguard against French aggression in the future. It will be noticed that it was limited to this special object, and differed widely from other schemes of alliance brought forward by Alexander at a later stage. Castlereagh had his own ideas as to a wider application of the ideas of 'alliance' and 'guarantee', but these were always subordinated to the special alliance against France, which must first be secured at all costs.

He had also other objects which were not so susceptible of being made into definite instructions. There is no hint in this Memorandum of the dethronement of Napoleon. Yet most of the Cabinet, supported by public opinion in England, were desirous of attaining this object. Castlereagh himself appreciated, however, the dangers of such an attempt, and as yet he was prepared to make peace with Napoleon if he could obtain a satisfactory one, though he was ready to work for the restoration of the Bourbons if an opportunity presented itself. Secondly, it was his desire, and that of his Cabinet, if possible, to confine France strictly to her 'ancient limits', those of pre-Revolutionary France. But here again he could not, as yet, press for too much. Part of Belgium and the left bank of the Rhine, as well as Savoy, might have to be surrendered. The extension of Holland was to depend on the wishes of the Great Powers. The desire that France should give up all her conquests is, however, clearly indicated in a 'Memorandum on the Maritime Peace', which is contained in the same volume as the instructions. In this it is clearly stated that the restoration of the French colonies should depend, if possible, upon the reduction of France to her 'ancient limits' as well as on an amicable arrangement among the Allies as to their own possessions.

This last point was one of special importance. Castlereagh knew that the peace of Europe depended as much on an amicable arrangement among the Allies touching their own possessions as on the treaty to be made with France. He was well aware of the dissensions between Austria and Russia on the subjects of Poland and Saxony, and he was subsequently forced to devote himself as much to the solution of these difficulties as to the treaty of peace with the enemy. It was his opinion that a lasting peace could only be obtained if a real balance of power were established in Europe; and he was afraid that the plans of Alexander might make this impossible. These were objects, however, on which he did not find it possible at the moment of the final conflict with France to lay down express conditions. He reserved them to be dealt with as circumstances might dictate. His first task was to attain the objects of special interest to Great Britain, but at the same time he knew that it would be necessary for him to act as mediator between the Allies on the points of dispute between them.

Section 5. *First Conferences at Bâle and Langres*

The relations between Alexander and Metternich had been still more embittered by a dispute as to the passage of the Allied troops through Switzerland. The Tsar was now also actively

supporting Bernadotte's pretensions to the throne of France;
and no plan had been made either for carrying on military
operations against Napoleon or for discussing with him a treaty
of peace. Castlereagh's arrival was awaited with the keenest
anxiety by the rival Powers, for they knew that on his decisions
their future conduct would depend.[1] Having at The Hague
settled to his satisfaction with the Prince of Orange the delicate
matters of the marriage, the Dutch barrier, and the colonies,
Castlereagh proceeded to Bâle, where he arrived on January
18, 1814. Alexander had been obliged to leave, but Castlereagh
found a note awaiting him entreating him not to make up
his mind until he had met the Emperor. Castlereagh had,
however, immediately interviews with Metternich, Stadion,
and Hardenberg. The Austrian Ministers were loud in their
complaints of Alexander's intrigues with Bernadotte, and
Metternich declared point-blank that the Austrian army would
refuse to march unless the Tsar's project was abandoned; while
the Prussians were on his side in this matter. Metternich further
declared that, while Austria was prepared to renounce all the
advantages of her dynastic connection with Napoleon in
favour of the Bourbons, if circumstances permitted, neither
her pride nor her interests could allow a French general to be
placed with the help of Alexander on the throne of France.
With this point of view Castlereagh was in full agreement;
but he subsequently won Metternich's consent to the proposition that there really existed no middle course between
Bonaparte and the Bourbons, thus using the Austrian objection
to Bernadotte to bring about the abandonment of the idea of a
regency under Marie-Louise.[2]

[1] Cathcart to Castlereagh, Jan. 8, 1814, *Correspondence*, IX, 249; Metternich
to Schwarzenberg, Jan. 16, 1814; Klinkowström, *Oesterreichs Theilnahme
an den Befreiungskriegen*, p. 797.
[2] Castlereagh to Liverpool, Jan. 22, 1814, F.O. Continent Archives, 2.
    In a private letter to Liverpool of the same date, Castlereagh pointed out
that, while Great Britain could not take up the cause of the Bourbons

Castlereagh then proceeded to consider with Metternich and Hardenberg the method of negotiation with France. After a delay of nearly a month, Caulaincourt, the French Foreign Minister, had been invited to Châtillon, where a conference with the enemy was to take place; and the Allies were already pledged to a discussion of peace terms. The Ministers in this discussion at Bâle had therefore immediately to consider how far France was to be allowed to influence, or even to be informed of, the disposition of the conquered territory. At previous discussions at Prague and at Frankfurt Napoleon had clearly shown that it was his intention to claim a voice in the shaping of Central Europe, and he hoped to use the rivalries of the Allies for his own purposes, and thus to produce a peace much more favourable to France. At Prague such a demand could not well be refused, but after Leipzig the Allies were resolved to keep these matters in their own hands. Castlereagh now found that it was determined to

'exclude France practically, but in the least offensive way, from any interference in the arrangements beyond her own limits'.

and that the Tsar was especially insistent on this point, and even wished that Napoleon should be refused all information on the subject. To Castlereagh, however, this proposal appeared to be too great an insult to French pride. He therefore hoped that

'the relative shape of Europe, at least in outline, as proposed by the Allies, might be presented to the enemy at the same time as the proposition as to his own limits was tendered to him'.

Napoleon might then fairly be called upon to give an answer within the specified time. This, of course, meant that the Allies must at once settle their own differences, and Castlereagh hoped to achieve this end at once, so that a complete scheme

without prejudicing her position in other matters, yet it might be possible for the Bourbon Princes to make efforts on their own behalf in order to make their cause more prominent.—*Correspondence* IX, 186.

might be presented to France. That this view was far too optimistic was soon to become apparent, but as yet none of the Powers realised that the problems before them were so complex that they would take eighteen months to solve.[1]

With regard to the boundaries of France, Castlereagh made considerable progress in the direction of reducing the terms to be offered to the 'ancient limits'. He induced Metternich to agree that both Luxemburg and Mainz must be taken from France, and the erection of a barrier in the Netherlands was also agreed to, though its exact extent could not yet be determined. Austria had decided to abandon the Netherlands and to refuse any compensation on the left bank of the Rhine.[2] Castlereagh, who wanted effective support for Holland by a Great Power, therefore began to look to Prussia to act as the guardian of the western frontier of Germany.[3] The chief importance of this first meeting lies, however, in the harmonious relations established between Castlereagh and Metternich. The latter was completely won over, though he had but just declared that the objects of the Coalition were already achieved, and had refused to allow the Austrian armies to march. His despatches to his trusted subordinate, Hudelist, were full of praise of Castlereagh;[4] and, feeling now less afraid

---

[1] Castlereagh to Liverpool, Jan. 22, 1814; Wellington, *Supplementary Despatches*, VIII, 537.

[2] Metternich had already refused Alsace, which Alexander had proposed that Austria should take in exchange for Galicia.—Fournier, *Napoleon I*, Eng. edn., II, 340.

[3] Castlereagh to Liverpool, Jan. 22, 1814, W.S.D., VIII, 537. 'I was induced to throw out the idea of thus bringing forward Prussia, as I recollected it was a favourite scheme of Pitt. . . I doubt much the policy of making Holland a Power of the first order, to which she would approach if she possessed the whole of these territories.' Hanoverian interests were not without influence in this decision. Münster was much afraid lest Holland should become a dangerous rival to Hanover. Münster to the Prince Regent, Feb. 19, 1814. Hanover Archives.

[4] Metternich to Hudelist, Jan. 17, 20, 21, 1814. Fournier, *Congress von Châtillon*, pp. 250 ff.

of Alexander, he was ready to continue the war against Napoleon. He also flattered himself that Castlereagh had fallen under his influence. In this, however, he was mistaken. Castlereagh's view, expressed to Liverpool a month later, showed that, while he wished to co-operate with Metternich, whom he regarded as the most practical of the European statesmen, he was not blind to his demerits.[1]

The two Ministers, having thus established a preliminary agreement, proceeded from Bâle to headquarters at Langres, where the whole matter had to be thrashed out with Alexander. It was Castlereagh who immediately took the lead in the discussions. His first task was to attack Alexander on the question of the candidature of Bernadotte. Alexander, while he asserted that he would take no steps in favour of Bernadotte, revealed an intense hostility to the restoration of the Bourbons, and expressed his intention of leaving the French to choose whom they liked. The Tsar was also at first determined to press on to Paris at all costs; while the Austrians, diplomatists and soldiers alike, held the view that, as complete victory was not certain, it was better to get a good peace while they could. It was Castlereagh's object to harmonise these points of view by insisting both on the forward march of the operations and the opening of peace discussions. If Napoleon refused terms which would now be considerably more stringent than those offered at Frankfurt, then he felt sure of persuading Metternich to go as far as was necessary. Meanwhile, Alexander must consent to negotiate.

On January 29 the Ministers of the four Powers met to endorse these decisions by a written agreement, which is

[1] Castlereagh to Liverpool, Feb. 26, 1814. F.O. Continent Archives 2. 'He is constitutionally temporising; he is charged with more faults than belong to him, but he has his full share, mixed up, however, with considerable means for carrying forward the machine, more than any other person I have met with at headquarters.' See an article on their relations in *Transactions Royal Hist. Soc.*, 3rd series, vol. VI.

known as the Langres Protocol. It was agreed that there should be no suspension of operations, and that Schwarzenberg should have a free hand to direct them as he liked. With regard to the offer to be made to France, Castlereagh insisted that the progress of the Allied armies and the defection of Murat entitled them to demand a peace which substantially reduced France to her 'ancient limits'.[1] He carried his point after much discussion, and was able to report that 'we may now be considered as practically delivered from the embarrassments of the Frankfurt negotiations'. He also insisted that France must be informed, so far as possible, of the method by which the Powers intended to dispose of their conquests, though she was to have no right to interfere in their disposal. His insistence that all question of maritime rights must be entirely excluded from discussion, and France so informed at the outset, was at once accepted. Finally, he made it clear that, while he was ready to make peace with Napoleon, this disposition depended on the latter retaining the support of his subjects, and that the restoration of the Bourbons was regarded by him as the inevitable consequence of Napoleon's fall. This frank conference, which was resumed on three succeeding days, produced an immediate diminution of the tension between the Allies 'owing to the natural vent which this species of Cabinet has afforded to the diverging sentiments of the respective Governments'.[2] Their decisions were embodied in the instructions drawn up for the representatives they intended to send to Châtillon to meet Caulaincourt, in which the 'ancient limits', with possible modifications, were laid down as the basis of negotiation.[3] Less satisfactory was the explanation to be given to Caulaincourt as

---

[1] Protocol of Jan. 29, 1814. The 'ancient limits' were to be offered, but modifications of them were to be discussed. Oncken, *Lord Castlereagh und die Ministerconferenz zu Langres, Historisches Taschenbuch*, VI, 3, p. 34; *Sbornik of the Russian Imperial Historical Society*, XXXI, 360.

[2] Castlereagh to Liverpool, Feb. 1, 1814, F.O. Continent 2.

[3] Fournier, *Congress von Châtillon*, p. 306.

to the future arrangement of Europe, which was in the vaguest terms. The restoration of Holland, 'with an increase of territory and a suitable frontier', was, however, specially mentioned; and this had been the main point in Castlereagh's instructions. All discussion of the maritime code was also, of course, to be excluded from the peace negotiations. Castlereagh had thus made great progress in obtaining what he had set out to win. He had also succeeded in obtaining some sort of harmony in the Alliance by at once taking the lead in all diplomatic and even military questions, and forcing, so far as possible, a decision on his Allies.[1]

Section 6. *The Châtillon Conference*

At the Châtillon Conference, which extended from February 4 to March 19, Napoleon was represented by the sincere and devoted Caulaincourt, whose eager desire for peace stands out in marked contrast to the cynical attitude of the Allied plenipotentiaries. But his master never yielded entirely to the entreaties of his Minister; and thus the exact course of the negotiations need not be entered into, since for the most part the conferences were without real substance. This Conference, however, provides an interesting precedent for a Peace Conference sitting while hostilities are still proceeding. The disposition of one side or the other to compromise depended to a great extent on the position in the field. The two sides were, however, so far from agreement at the outset that no peace would have possibly resulted. Napoleon, the heir of the Revolution, could not sign a peace which brought back France to the boundaries of the *ancien régime*. His victories in the middle of February made him obdurate; and even in March, when these successes had been shown to be only ephemeral, he could not bring himself to sign a peace which would leave France smaller than he found it. For Castlereagh the Conference

[1] Oncken, *Historisches Taschenbuch*, VI, 4, p. 36.

was mainly important in the effect which it was likely to produce on France and on Europe. He wished the onus of the continuance of the war to be thrown on Napoleon and not on the Allies. That he attached considerable importance to the method by which the negotiations were conducted is shown by the fact that he alone of the principal Ministers attended any portion of the conferences, though he left the actual conduct of the negotiations to his subordinates. The delegates nominated by the other Powers were all men of second rank.

It was soon apparent that some central control was needed. The Russian plenipotentiary, Razumoffski, had received orders from the Tsar to delay peace as long as possible,[1] this being Alexander's method of escaping from the obligations of the Langres Protocol; and the other plenipotentiaries were, for one reason or another, not likely to keep him in check.[2] As a result of Blücher's success at La Rothière on February 1, Alexander, without consulting his allies, sent a peremptory order for the negotiations to be suspended. Castlereagh, at the urgent request of Metternich, hurried back to re-establish the concert, and on his return had again to leave when the successes of Napoleon had produced a new crisis. In these circumstances, the negotiations were largely a duel of words. Caulaincourt demanded in vain to know the plans which the Allies had made for Germany and Italy. This was just what the Allies could not tell him, since they had not agreed amongst themselves. They were only decided that such matters were no concern of France, and reiterated the question. Would France accept or not the return to the 'ancient limits', or something like them? These terms Caulaincourt could not get his master to accept; and, as

---

[1] *Sbornik of the Russian Imperial Historical Society*, XXXI. 370.
[2] Stadion, the Austrian, was opposed to Metternich's plans, Humboldt, the Prussian, simply wanted revenge on France, and none of the English plenipotentiaries were men of diplomatic ability.

soon as the Treaty of Chaumont, which was signed on March 9, had terminated the internal difficulties of the Alliance, the negotiations were ordered to be broken off.

'I wish it had been possible,' reported Castlereagh, 'with less sacrifice in point of time to have ascertained, in a manner that would satisfy the world of the fact, the impracticability of concluding peace with the existing ruler of France; but it has, at length, been accomplished in a manner which I am persuaded can leave no reasonable doubt in the view even of the French nation.'[1]

Section 7. The Maintenance of the Alliance

Castlereagh's principal task was to keep the Alliance together while the issue was still in doubt, and to construct a treaty which should provide for the security of Europe after the war. There were two occasions, at least, when it seemed that he had failed, in spite of the promising opening of his negotiations at Langres. The first was on the suspension of the negotiations at Châtillon on February 8. Alexander thought he could march straight to Paris, dethrone Bonaparte, and set up any claimant whom he regarded as likely to win the support of the French. Castlereagh hurried to headquarters, and had two long and very stormy interviews with the Tsar, in which he stressed the dangers of making the fall of Napoleon the direct object of the war.[2] He pointed out that it was one thing to take Paris as a natural result of military operations; it was another to go there to set up a new government the character of which was not yet determined. In Castlereagh's view, such a new government could only be the Bourbons, but he urged that there was, as yet, no sign that the French wanted them back, in spite of the fact that Allied armies were on French soil. He asked the Tsar:

---

[1] Castlereagh to Liverpool, Mar. 22, 1814, F.O. Continent 3.
[2] Castlereagh to Liverpool, Feb. 16, 1814, F.O. Continent 3.

'how long he would undertake to *keep his army* in France to fight
the battles of a Bourbon against Bonaparte, and whether his
Allies would engage for theirs',

and what would be the attitude of the French people towards
a sovereign whom the Allies, rejecting a peace on their own
terms, had forced on them at the point of the bayonet. He
told the Emperor that the Ministerial Council had considered
the matter that morning, and that they felt that Alexander's
idea was

'full of hazard, at direct variance with the principle upon which
the confederacy had been cemented amongst the Allies and
supported by Europe, and that they feared it might lead to failure,
disgrace, and disunion'.

Alexander could make no reply to this attack; but he attempted
to refute Castlereagh by denying that he really represented the
opinions of his Government or his people. The Tory press
was, as he knew, loud against Bonaparte and in favour of the
Bourbons. But, further than this, the Prince Regent and the
Prime Minister had been indiscreet in their conversations with
Lieven, the Russian Ambassador. Alexander now endeavoured
to use the wishes of the Prince Regent, as reported by Lieven,
as a means of weakening Castlereagh's opposition.[1] It was not
the last occasion on which this game was played, but it made
no impression, either now or later, on the Foreign Minister. He
claimed full powers to act as he wished, denied Alexander's
right to question it, and sent Robinson home post-haste to
bring back definite instructions that he had full support, and
to stop all such intrigues in the future. He told his Cabinet
plainly that he would never support a war prolonged merely to
dethrone Bonaparte if other objects were secured, however

[1] Castlereagh to Liverpool, Feb. 18, 1814, enclosing Lieven to Nesselrode,
Jan. 26, 1814, *Correspondence*, IX, 226. See also Princess Lieven's acoount
in her diary in the Grand Duke Nicholas Michaelovitch's *Correspondence
de l'Empereur Alexandre avec sa Soeur la Grande-Duchesse Catharine*, p. 226.

much he would welcome his fall if it were brought about by the natural sequence of events. Liverpool, of course, gave him full support, and though there was some difficulty with the Prince Regent and some members of the Cabinet, instructions such as Castlereagh had requested were sent to him to strengthen his position.[1] The result was that he secured a continuance of the negotiations with Napoleon which the Allies had, as yet, no excuse for breaking off. New instructions were sent from Allied Headquarters to Châtillon which went still further in the direction of the 'ancient limits', with corresponding cessions of colonies, while France was to be expressly excluded from intervening in the disposition of the conquered territories.[2]

'What will be the fate of the whole, I cannot guess,' wrote Castlereagh, 'but we have acted consistently and honourably; and if we are still exposed to Bonaparte, with a defensive alliance (upon which I have made useful progress) and such a peace we need not trouble for the future.'

The second occasion on which Castlereagh had to intervene to save the Coalition from dissolution was almost immediately after this decision. Napoleon's victories of February 8-10 over Blücher had had the effect of making Alexander more reasonable. Those of February 17, 18, and 21 against Schwarzenberg, which forced the main Allied army to retreat, turned his self-confidence into something like panic. On the 18th

---

[1] Bathurst to Castlereagh, Feb. 7, 1814, F.O. Continent Archives 2. Liverpool spoke very strongly to Lieven on the use that had been made of the Ambassador's letter. According to the Russian Ambassador, Bathurst, Harrowby, and Eldon were strongly against a peace with Napoleon. Lieven to Nesselrode, Mar. 1, 1814, Petrograd Archives. The Prussian Ambassador reported that it was only with the greatest difficulty that the Prince Regent's predilections for the Bourbons were overcome, and that the Cabinet was very divided. Jacobi to Hardenberg, Feb. 18, 1814, Berlin Archives. Liverpool and Sidmouth, however, threatened to resign if the Prince Regent persisted. Wessenberg to Metternich, Feb. 15, 1814, Vienna Archives.

[2] D'Angeberg, *Le Congrès de Vienne*, p. 111.

Schwarzenberg, with the assent of Alexander and the King of Prussia, thought it well to ask for an armistice rather than risk a decisive battle. Castlereagh learnt of the fact at Châtillon, whither he had returned to set the negotiations in train on the basis of the new instructions, by a letter from Metternich to Stadion which hinted that peace must be made.[1] He made immediately an indignant protest in a letter to Metternich.[2] He then hurried to headquarters, where he found an alarming situation. The recriminations between Austria and Russia were at their height, and Castlereagh confessed that his patience was almost worn out in dealing with them both. Austria in the depths of despair, was eager for peace; and Alexander, who considered that he had been betrayed by the Austrians, was now also ready to give way.[3] Each Power, indeed, suspected

[1] Metternich to Stadion, Feb. 18, 1814. Metternich had, however, not been consulted before the offer was made. Fournier, *Congress von Châtillon*, p. 324.

[2] Castlereagh to Metternich, Feb. 18, 1814, F.O. Continent Archives 2; 'I cannot express to you how much I regret the proposition of armistice. . . . An offer so inconsistent with the proceedings here, and of so little dignity in itself, cannot fail to invite the enemy to assume a tone of authority. I feel it more than ever necessary to conjure you and your colleagues at headquarters not to suffer yourselves to descend from the substance of your peace. You owe it, such as you have announced it to the enemy, to yourselves and to Europe, and you will now more than ever make a fatal sacrifice, both of moral and political impression, if, under the pressure of these slight reverses, which are incident to war, and some embarrassments in your Council which I should hope are at an end, the great edifice of peace was suffered to be disfigured in its proportions. . . . If we act with military and political prudence, how can France resist a just peace demanded by 600,000 warriors? Let her if she dare; and the day you can declare that fact to the French nation, rest assured Bonaparte is subdued.' See also Oncken, *Die Krisis der letzten Friedensverhandlung mit Napoleon I, Historisches Taschenbuch*, VI, 5, 48.

[3] Castlereagh to Liverpool, Feb. 26, 1814, F.O. Continent 3; 'The Emperor was the first to descend from the project of Paris to that of armistice, and I received last night a message from His Imperial Majesty by Count Nesselrode, probably embroidered by the bearer, to urge the expedience of an early peace. But I do not altogether despair of his perseverance, and if I can get him to speak out to Austria and allay all her alarms, real or pretended, I am confident she could not leave us upon the main question. . . . The

that the others was trying to keep its army intact in order to influence future decisions as to the division of the spoils.[1] Castlereagh only succeeded in reuniting the Alliance by a great effort. He told the Allies that Great Britain would never restore her conquests unless she got a peace on the Continent such as she desired.

'Nothing keeps either Power firm but the consciousness that without Great Britain the peace cannot be made. They have all been lowering their tone to me, but I have explicitly told them that if the Continent can and will make a peace with Bonaparte upon a principle of authority, for such a peace Great Britain will make the greatest sacrifices. But if they neither will nor can, we must, for their sake as well as our own, rest in position against France. . . . Whatever may be the issue, I have thought our line, to do any good, must be a decided one, and I have represented to them all the hopelessness of their future security against France re-established if they shrink now from the contest when they are reunited.'

At the same time, he took energetic measures to strengthen the military position. At his suggestion troops were detached from Bernadotte's force and given to Blücher, 'who is too daring to be trusted with a small army, but a host at the head of 100,000 men', and an attack on Antwerp by the Swedes was ordered. He also proposed that a Military Commission should be formed to investigate the exact number of the Allied forces and prepare a plan of campaign.[2] In short, by pointing out to the Allies the real strength of their position, by allaying their

Emperor of Russia, not quite satisfied with himself, is loud against the Austrians for not giving battle, and told me that Schwarzenberg had secret orders from his Court not to fight a general action in the then state of the negotiations.'

[1] Münster to the Prince Regent, Feb. 25, 1814; 'Je ne doute pas que les Autrichiens songent à tenir leur armée intacte, afin de conserver leur influence sur les affaires de Pologne; de l'autre côté, on accuse les Russes de ménager leur belle cavalerie.' Fournier, *op cit.*, p. 303.

[2] Castlereagh to Liverpool, Mar. 4, 1814, F.O. Continent 3.

D

mutual suspicions, and especially by showing them that he held the key to peace in the colonial conquests, which he would only use if he was satisfied with the Continental position, he succeeded in reconstructing the Alliance and bringing it once more to energetic action.

Section 8. The Treaty of Chaumont. The Construction of The Quadruple Alliance

A treaty had, however, yet to be made; and these two incidents had shown how necessary it was. Castlereagh had already submitted his proposals for a defensive alliance to the Ministers of the Great Powers, and secured their general approval.[1] Now he wanted to complete this treaty, which should give complete security against France in the future, and at the same time obtain the objects which Great Britain had most at heart. He had already made his subsidy proposals conditional on the separation of the Netherlands from France. For on Antwerp he knew that Napoleon would insist to the very last; and it was therefore all the more important to bind his Allies to go on until this object were attained.[2] At last, on March 9, the Treaty of Chaumont was signed. The four Powers bound themselves to continue the war until their objects were attained. These objects were, as defined in secret articles, a confederated Germany, an independent Switzerland, an Italy comprised of separate independent States, a free Spain under the Bourbon House, and an enlarged Holland, of which the Prince of Orange was to be Sovereign. All the other articles except this last were matters, of course, on which there was no dispute. The aggrandisement of Holland was the main instruction given to Castlereagh, and he here obtained it by treaty from the Allies. For this he had indeed to pay heavily. In money

[1] Castlereagh to Liverpool, Feb. 18, 1814, F.O. Continent 3.
[2] Castlereagh to Liverpool, Mar. 4, 1814, F.O. Continent 3.

and men combined England's contribution was to be twice as large as that of each Continental Power.

But Castlereagh also secured the other point of his instructions, on which, perhaps, he laid more stress than on anything else. The Alliance was to continue for twenty years after war had ceased, and the Powers were to protect one another against any attempt by France to upset the arrangements made in the forthcoming peace. This was the origin of the Quadruple Alliance which was to dominate European politics for thirty years and far outlast its purpose. It was made under the strain of the overwhelming military superiority which France had obtained under the Napoleonic régime, and the helplessness of all the rest of Continental Europe against her, except in combination. The object, therefore, as laid down in Article XVI of the treaty, was to secure 'the balance of power': and, though there were to be many changes in the attitude of the various Powers during the next eighteen months, this idea persisted to the end of the European settlement, and on the whole may have been said to have been achieved. The treaty was intended, as Castlereagh told his Government, to be regarded

> 'not only as a systematic pledge of persevering concert amongst the leading Powers, but a refuge under which all the minor States, especially those on the Rhine, may look forward to find their security upon the return of peace relieved of the necessity of seeking a compromise with France'.[1]

It was, in fact, to be a League of Nations against France, to which all Powers, great and small, could look for protection. This device, invented by Castlereagh himself, and forced by him on the Allies, is perhaps his greatest achievement and title to fame. How hard it was to construct it has been shown in the preceding pages.

[1] Castlereagh to Liverpool, Mar. 10, 1814, F.O. Continent 3. Spain, Portugal, Sweden, and Holland were to be invited to accede.

Section 9. The Problem of the Conquered Territories

But, though he had secured the Alliance, the barrier in the Netherlands, and practically the left bank of the Rhine—though, that is, the boundaries of France had been largely determined—little progress had yet been made in settling the claims of the three Continental Powers, which had been at the bottom of all their recriminations and disputes. Ceaseless negotiations had taken place amongst the Ministers of the Powers on this point, and a plan was already being drawn up; but nothing definite had yet matured. The exact course of events is not easy to trace, since there are few official transactions, and each Minister was moving with extreme caution, uncertain alike of the course he ought to pursue and what were the real intentions of his Allies. The only point on which the Great Powers were really in agreement was that they were to settle these matters among themselves, and that neither France nor the smaller European States were to do more than acquiesce in their decisions. It had already been arranged at Langres that a Congress should be held at Vienna, which the three Sovereigns promised to attend in person; and a formal invitation was procured from the town of Vienna for that purpose.[1] But this Congress was meant merely to ratify decisions previously made by the Great Powers, and these decisions it was intended to make at the earliest opportunity. They were, at any rate, to be incorporated in the peace treaty with France, so that her signature might be obtained before the meeting of the Congress.

Castlereagh was exceedingly anxious to settle these questions, which he could perceive were exercising a profound and dangerous influence on the progress of the war, and he was at no

[1] Münster to the Prince Regent, Feb. 2, 1814, Hanover Archives. As to why Vienna was chosen for the meeting-place of the Congress see the paper on International Congresses. Details as to the discussions on this point are lacking. Not only, however, was Vienna in a convenient central position, but the attitude of mediator which Metternich had assumed in 1813 had caused the Austrian capital to be considered as the natural locality for such an assembly.

loss to decide where British interests lay. The foundation of all the subsequent negotiations lies in a verbal agreement between Metternich and Hardenberg, made early in January, that Austria would agree to Prussia's claims on Saxony if Prussia would unite with Austria to defeat Alexander's plans for the creation of a Polish kingdom.[1] Castlereagh, who had inherited from Pitt an extreme distrust of Russia, from the first made this agreement the foundation of his diplomacy. It suited his policy in two particulars. He was anxious to make Prussia a strong and united State, so that she might play her part in re-establishing the territorial equilibrium which it was his main object to produce, and he wished to keep Russia as far as possible from Central Europe.

Alexander, however, regarded the creation of a Kingdom of Poland as already settled. In January, indeed, he promised Cathcart that he would not press his claims on Prussian Poland, but this promise was not seriously meant.[2] To Austria he first proposed that she should take Alsace from France, and cede him the whole of Galicia.[3] In February, it is true, he was prepared to accept only Western Galicia, over which he declared Austria had no claim: but beyond this he would not go. Czartoryski was received at headquarters, and there were rumours that he would replace Nesselrode. Castlereagh threw his whole weight on the other side. He told the Austrians that he was in entire agreement with them on the subject of Poland,[4] and at the beginning of March he had an interview with Czartoryski and Radziwill.[5]

[1] Hardenberg's *Tagebuch*, Jan. 8, 1814. Fournier, *Congress von Châtillon*, p. 361. See also Cathcart to Castlereagh, Jan. 16, 1814, *Correspondence*, IX, 171.
[2] Cathcart to Castlereagh, as above.
[3] Munster to the Prince Regent Feb. 23, 25, 1814. Fournier, *Congress von Châtillon*, pp. 302, 303.
[4] Stadion to Metternich, Feb. 9, 1814. Fournier, *Zur Vorgeschichte des Wiener Kongresses*; *Hist. Studien und Skizzen*, II, 297.
[5] Castlereagh to Liverpool, Mar, 3, 1814, F.O. Continent 3.

'I hope I have succeeded,' he wrote, 'in discrediting their views, considering them in truth a diversion in favour of France; the former, who is a person both of principle and merit, promised to absent himself from the headquarters if his presence was considered as calculated to create disunion, which I ventured with every possible sentiment of regard to assure him was the fact.'

No impression was, however, made on the Tsar, who remained in constant communication with Czartoryski, and no progress could be made towards an agreement.

Other points were under constant discussion among the Allied Ministers. As has been seen, the aggrandisement of Holland and the independence of Switzerland and Spain had been put into treaty form. As to Germany, all that had been decided was that it should be composed of independent States united in a 'lien fédératif'.[1] This federal Constitution had, however, been already much discussed, and the bases of it laid at Langres in January;[2] and a draft scheme was drawn up on March 10 by Stein, with the assistance of Humboldt. In this matter Castlereagh himself took little part, either now or later, Münster being used to represent the British Government as well as Hanover. More important from the present point of view was, however, the territorial distribution. But though the outlines of a scheme gradually appeared, everything depended on the Saxon question, and, as the settlement of this depended on the Polish one, no decisions could be made. As to Italy, it had been generally agreed that Austria should be compensated there, but, though the treaty with Murat had, temporarily at least, settled the south, the disposition of the States of the north could not yet be decided.[3]

[1] Münster, p. 160.

[2] In Oct. 1813 England had urged Austria to assume once more the Imperial Crown, but Metternich had refused. Oncken, *Aus den letzten Monaten des Jahres 1813. Historisches Taschenbuch*, VI, 2, p. 66.

[3] The Cabinet were dissatisfied that Castlereagh had not made the establishment of Sardinia a special point of the Chaumont Treaty, but the latter pointed out that the omission was intentional on his part, 'the object of

Here again, then, only a vague principle had been recognised.

Section 10. The Allies and the Restoration of the Bourbons

The question whether Napoleon was to remain on the throne of France, and, if not, who was to succeed him, had always underlain all these discussions. Castlereagh's position, as has been shown, was that peace must be made with Napoleon if he would consent to the 'ancient limits'. But he did not expect him to do so, and in that case he wished the Bourbons to return. He would not be a party, however, to any overt attempt to set up the Bourbons while the Allies were still in negotiation with the Emperor, and he was confirmed in this view by the absence of any signs that the French people were ready of their own will to dethrone Bonaparte or welcome back the ancient family.[1] His cabinet were, reluctantly for the most part, forced to support this point of view, but they grew more and more restive as time went on and peace and final victory were still delayed. Public opinion in England grew more and more vehement in favour of the overthrow of Napoleon, though Liverpool himself distrusted the Bourbons, and took all steps to prevent the imprudence of the Prince Regent from committing British policy.[2] The Bourbon Princes at last began to act, and the Comte d'Artois went to Switzerland in February,[3] while the Duc d'Angoulême went to the south

that instrument not being to declare a comprehensive arrangement for the Continent, but to secure on the part of Great Britain the points most essential to her honour and interest.' He had, therefore, wished 'to avoid swelling the catalogue of special concessions by including in it objects otherwise secured.' Castlereagh to Liverpool, Mar. 5, 1814, F.O. Continent 3.

[1] Castlereagh to Liverpool, Mar. 4, 1814, F.O. Continent 3.
[2] Liverpool to Wellington, Feb. 9, *Wellington*; *Supplementary Despatches*, VIII, 580.
[3] See the correspondence of the Comte d'Artois—'Monsieur'—with Alexander, in *Wellington*; *Supplementary Despatches*, VIII, 619.

and the Duc de Berri to Brittany. At Paris also Talleyrand and others were already thinking of the Bourbons; but no communication with the Allies was established until the Châtillon Conference was dissolved and Napoleon had refused the terms offered.

Thus it was not until March 22 that Castlereagh was able to report the appearance of a secret envoy at headquarters. This envoy, Baron Vitrolles, had set out in March, but was not received until after the Chaumont Treaty had been signed. He had then interviews with Metternich, who welcomed him, and Alexander, who told him that the Bourbons were unfit to govern France. Castlereagh, as soon as he knew of the definite breach of Châtillon, supported Metternich, and made preparations to bring the Bourbon Princes to headquarters, a confidential mission being sent to the Comte d'Artois in Switzerland for this purpose. By now Bordeaux had proclaimed its adhesion to the Bourbons; and Castlereagh thought the time had come to act. On March 28, at a dinner at Dijon, at which Castlereagh, Metternich, and Razumoffski were present, the Bourbons were publicly toasted by the Allied Ministers. Castlereagh did not wish, however, to play a very prominent part in this movement, but to leave the initiative to the Continental Powers.[1] In all this he only anticipated the intentions of the home Government. On March 19 instructions had been sent that the negotiations should be brought to an immediate close; while, on the receipt of the news that Bordeaux had declared for the Bourbons, Castlereagh was ordered not to be a party to any treaty with Napoleon.[2] The

[1] Castlereagh to Liverpool, Mar. 22, 30, 1814, F.O. Continent 3; 'The object I have in view . . . is to bring Great Britain forward in whatever may regard the interior of France rather as the ally and auxiliary of the Continental Powers than as charging herself in chief, and making herself responsible for what cannot be conducted under the superintendence of her own Government'

[2] Bathurst to Castlereagh, Mar. 19, 22, 1814, F.O. Continent Archives 1.

Cabinet were prepared to back the Bourbons now that part of France appeared to be on their side.

Section 11. *The Overthrow of Napoleon and the First Peace of Paris*

Thus at the final stage of the fight with Napoleon, England and Austria were eager that the Bourbons should be brought back, though Alexander was still hostile. The Allies were linked together by the Treaty of Chaumont; their different claims on the Napoleonic Empire, though unsettled, were postponed for the moment; their military machinery had been overhauled and improved. In short, under the energetic leadership of Castlereagh the Coalition had survived, and even profited from, a period of defeat. The Allies knew from intercepted letters the desperate plight of Napoleon. Peremptory orders were sent to Chaumont that the negotiations must be terminated.[1] Caulaincourt was even yet not able to obtain from Napoleon instructions that authorised him to make any approach towards the terms offered by the Allies. While he was still offering counter-projects which discussed the fate of Saxony and Italy, the farce was terminated; and on March 19 the Conference of Châtillon broke up, a manifesto to the French nation being issued on the 25th by the Allies, which laid the blame for the continuance of the war entirely on Napoleon. Five days later the Allies were at the gates of Paris; and Napoleon's last desperate effort to stave off his ruin was frustrated by the defection of his generals. On March 31, Alexander, accompanied by Frederick William, realised his long-cherished wish, and entered Paris as a conqueror, or, as he would have preferred to phrase it, as liberator.

Both the Emperor of Austria and Metternich, together with

[1] Instruction envoyée à Châtillon, Mar. 11, 1814. Fournier, *Congress von Châtillon*, p. 343.

Castlereagh, remained at Dijon. Francis II was not eager to appear as conqueror in the capital of his son-in-law. Nor was Castlereagh anxious to take part in the negotiations at Paris. He was convinced that the steps taken by himself, in conjunction with Metternich and Hardenberg, would result in a declaration for the Bourbons. Nesselrode was on their side and, in communication with Talleyrand, ready to check any move of Bernadotte or the Bonapartists.[1] Thus Alexander, who entered the city convinced that the Bourbon cause was without support, found there a vigorous and active Bourbon party, which Talleyrand, the most astute head in Europe, was leading. He had no alternative but to bring back to the French throne the Bourbons whom he detested and despised. He insisted, however, on the promise of a Constitution, and prevented the exiled King from returning as an absolute monarch.

Castlereagh from the first had intended to keep apart from these arrangements. A Convention between Austria, Russia, and Prussia had been signed so long ago as February 14 for the regulation of the procedure of the Allies in the event of a march to Paris, by which the Bourbons were to be proclaimed if there was sufficient popular support.[2] Alexander had seen, but not signed, this document; but he was now, much against his will, the instrument by which it was to be put into force. Castlereagh, though cognisant of all these matters, and largely inspiring them, refused to give any signature. He did not reach Paris till April 10, when the whole affair was over. His subordinates, who objected to Alexander playing the leading rôle, were urgent he should appear on the scene. But he had no wish to take a prominent part in a transaction which might

[1] Castlereagh to Liverpool, Dijon, Apr. 4, 1814, F.O. Continent Archives 2. A more general view is that Talleyrand planned the whole matter and convinced Alexander, but the evidence of the British Archives shows that Castlereagh and Metternich were quite assured as to the result.

[2] Oncken, *Das Zeitalter, etc.*, p. 769, from the Foreign Office Records.

give a considerable opportunity to the Opposition in the British Parliament. Similarly, he wanted to be not more than an acceding party to the Treaty of Fontainebleau, by which Napoleon was made sovereign of Elba; indeed, he seriously objected to the chivalrous terms which Alexander granted to his conquered foe.

These matters being settled, the Allied Ministers could proceed to draw up the Treaty of Peace with the Bourbon Government. The first step was to arrange for a cessation of hostilities which would free France from the Allied troops. Operations had now ceased except in the south of France, and by a convention of April 23 the Allies engaged to withdraw their forces from France in return for the surrender of the fortresses which were still held by French troops in Germany and Italy.[1] Louis XVIII returned to France on April 24, but the negotiations for the Treaty of Peace lasted till the end of May. Castlereagh, who was being constantly pressed to return home, was anxious to come to a conclusion as soon as possible, but, as he confessed to Bathurst, Paris was 'a bad place for business', and the balls, dinners, reviews, and fêtes did much to distract the Sovereigns and their Ministers from more serious work, a situation which pleased Talleyrand, who hoped to profit by the prolongation of the discussions. Eventually it was only by a threat to transfer the negotiations to London that Castlereagh obtained his signature to the treaty by the end of May.

The construction of the treaty with France raised, however, big problems which could not be disposed of without considerable expenditure of diplomatic energy. A Bourbon King could readily accept the ancient frontiers of France; but Talleyrand was anxious to obtain as much prestige as possible, both for himself and the restored monarchy. Castlereagh, who

[1] See the paper in this series on International Congresses, where the text is given.

considered that he had obtained from France the main securities necessary for the peace of Europe, was inclined to be liberal.[1] In his view he was supported to a considerable extent by Liverpool, who, like Castlereagh, had an eye to using French influence in the European settlement.[2] Thus, in refusing to demand a monetary indemnity from France such as Prussia desired (presenting for herself a bill of over one hundred million francs), or to allow the works of art of which Napoleon and his generals had plundered Europe to be restored to their owners, and in giving France a substantial increase on her 1792 boundaries, Castlereagh's influence was, in company with that of Alexander, on the side of generosity. When, however, Talleyrand attempted to take advantage of this attitude to refuse the cession of St. Lucia and Tobago, and to avoid all reference to the abolition of the slave trade, he was met with a peremptory negative. Still more indignant was Castlereagh when a strong movement arose, supported not only by the Napoleonic generals but even by the King, to extend the French frontier on the side of Belgium.[3] He told Talleyrand that no peace could last unless the French people gave up 'this false notion of Flanders being necessary to France'; and it made him the more determined to secure a full recognition of the frontiers of the Netherlands in the Treaty of Peace.[4]

With regard to the slave trade, both Castlereagh and his Cabinet were urged on by an almost fanatical public opinion in England. The trade had been abolished in the colonies

---

[1] Castlereagh to Liverpool, Apr. 19, 1814; 'I am myself inclined to a liberal line upon subordinate questions, having secured the Continent, the ancient family, and the leading features of our own peace.' *Correspondence*, IX. 474.

[2] Liverpool to Castlereagh, May 19, 1814, *W.S.D.*, IX, 89.

[3] Castlereagh to Liverpool, May 19, 1814, F.O. Continent 4.

[4] Castlereagh to Liverpool, May 23, 1814; 'I felt it of the first importance not to go to a Congress without having this most essential point acquiesced in by that Power.' F.O. Continent 4.

which we were now handing back to France. The French view was that England, having stocked her own colonies with labour, was anxious to prevent those of other Powers obtaining a similar advantage. Castlereagh was anxious to get the abolition recognised by all Europe; but it was more difficult to refuse a term of years of delay if the principle was conceded, since the British abolition was so recent. Eventually France agreed that the trade should be abolished after five years' delay, and undertook to support the general principle at the Congress.

The final result of the treaties, which were signed on May 30, was that France received the boundaries of 1792, with certain additions which extended her north-eastern frontier so as to include districts round Philippeville and Saarbruck, the fortress of Landau, and a considerable portion of Savoy. Further territories belonging to other Powers and *enclaves* in France, such as Mülhausen and Avignon, of which there were also many on the north-eastern frontier, were now incorporated in her territory under her full sovereignty. She regained also most of her colonies except Tobago, St. Lucia, and Mauritius and its dependencies; while she was restricted to commercial privileges in India, giving up all sovereign rights. She also recognised the British possession of Malta.[1]

Section 12. The Attempt at Paris to settle the Conquered Territories

These treaties, however, besides regulating the relations of France with Europe, mark also a stage in the discussion of the problems that still divided the Allies. Castlereagh had at first

---

[1] Separate treaties were signed between each of the belligerent Powers and France. Including that with Spain, who did not sign until July 20, 1814, there were thus seven treaties, which were identical as regards the main instrument, though they varied to some extent in the secret and additional articles, in which the stipulations as to the rest of Europe were recorded.

intended that the future of Europe should be decided in London after the signature of the treaty with France.[1] But it was later decided that the main points of the European settlement should be settled in Paris; and, if the Powers could have come to an agreement, the main provisions would have been incorporated in the treaty with France and the future Congress have been merely concerned with the ratification of these decisions. In this, however, as at Langres and Chaumont, those who hoped to effect a settlement proved to be oversanguine. But a determined and serious effort was now made. Hardenberg and Metternich, secure in the knowledge that Castlereagh would support them, wished to bind Russia to the recognition of their scheme before the treaty with France was signed.[2] Hardenberg, after long conferences with Stadion, who represented Metternich, produced a plan for the future arrangement of Europe. By this scheme all Saxony was to go to Prussia, as well as the left bank of the Rhine; while Austria received Tirol and compensation in Italy. The Duchy of Warsaw was to be partitioned in such a manner that, while Russia obtained the largest part, both Prussia and Austria received substantial shares, the latter especially retaining Cracow and the Tarnopol district, which had been ceded by her in 1809. Compensations for Bavaria, Baden, and Piedmont were all indicated, and the plan of a German Constitution such as had already been prepared at Langres, was added.[3]

On May 5 Hardenberg submitted this plan to Alexander,

[1] Castlereagh to Liverpool, Apr. 13, 1814, *Correspondence*, IX, 460.

[2] Castlereagh to Liverpool, May 5, 1814; 'A strong desire felt by Prussia and Austria to bring both Russia and France to some understanding upon the main principles of the Continental arrangements in a secret article or otherwise previous to our stipulating away our conquests has led to a tedious and elaborate examination of this very complicated and arduous question.' F.O. Continent 4.

[3] Hardenberg's plan 'pour l'arrangement futur de l'Europe' in F.O. Continent 4. Described by Münster, *Political Sketches*, p. 159, and Treitschke, *History of Germany* (English edition), I, 661.

but met with a peremptory refusal. Not only was the Tsar unwilling to cede territory to Austria, but he persisted in pressing for an extension of the western frontier of Poland, so as to include Thorn and a large *rayon* beyond it. The Polish question thus reached a deadlock. The agreement between Austria and Prussia was also an uneasy one; for, though Metternich was prepared to give Saxony to Prussia, he insisted that she should not obtain Mainz, the great fortress of Southern Germany, which was greatly coveted by the Prussian generals. Prussian troops now took possession of this place, a proceeding at which Austria was highly indignant; and the question of Mainz was to be a great stumbling-block to peace until the end. A final settlement as to Germany had, therefore, to be postponed until the London Conferences, though Stein was eager to get all signed at Paris, and attempted to get Alexander to insist on it.[1] The uncertainty of the territorial settlement was, indeed, felt by all to be a great disadvantage. All Powers were eager to enter into provisional occupation of the countries which would fall to their share; and meanwhile in the territories that were likely to change hands there was the utmost confusion and grave acts of tyranny on the part of masters who felt that their reign of power was to be brief.

On May 21 Metternich, Hardenberg, and Münster again attempted to come to a settlement, but in vain. On the Polish question also, at the last moment, Alexander urged that a decision should be made;[1] but Metternich and Castlereagh by this time thought it more likely that settlement on these lines would be reached in London, where Polish influence was not so strong as in Paris, and this matter was also postponed.[2]

When the Peace of Paris was signed it contained, therefore, only the recognition of a small part of the European settlement. The incorporation of the Low Countries with Holland was agreed to, as well as the restoration of the King of Sardinia to

[1] Münster, *op. cit.*, pp. 169, 171.   [2] Münster, *op. cit.*, p. 184.

Piedmont, with which was to be incorporated Genoa (to remain a free port), while the frontier of the Austrian possessions in Italy, which gave her Lombardy and Venetia, were defined; as regards the territories ceded on the left bank of the Rhine it was simply stated that they should serve as compensations to Holland, Prussia, and other German States. The only articles devoted to general interests were those which recognised the principle of free navigation of international rivers,[1] and one containing a promise by France to support the abolition of the slave trade at the Congress. All the rest of the matters in dispute had to be postponed. It was agreed by Article XXXII of the public treaty that

> 'all the Powers engaged on either side in the present war shall within the space of two months send plenipotentiaries to Vienna for the purpose of regulating in General Congress the arrangements which are to complete the present treaty'.

But the four Powers, though unable to make express stipulations in the treaty, made it clear that they had no intention of allowing the decisions to be made by a general assembly of the European States. By a secret article France agreed that the disposition of the territories ceded by her, and

> 'the relations from whence a system of real and permanent balance of power in Europe is to be derived, shall be regulated at the Congress upon the principles determined upon by the Allied Powers amongst themselves'.

The Treaties of Paris were made with Portugal, Sweden, and Spain as well as the four Great Powers; but the latter did not intend the three smaller to have much share in the decision. It was still hoped to settle these matters before the Congress met in London, whither the Emperor of Russia, the King of Prussia, and their Ministers, as also Metternich, were now proceeding. It cannot too often be insisted on that, throughout

---

[1] Fournier, *Zur Vorgeschichte des Wiener Congresses, Hist. Studien und Skizzen*, II, 299.

the whole of these negotiations, *the future Congress was intended to be only a ratifying instrument of the decisions of the four Great Powers.* The signing of the first Peace of Paris marks, however, a very definite stage in the transactions. In spite of all their endeavours, the Powers had not been able to come to an agreement before France secured liberty of action by signing the treaty. They had thus been unable to bind her to recognise the distribution of the spoils. Had Hardenberg's plan resulted in agreement, it is certain that the territorial arrangement of Germany would have been included as a secret article in the treaty in the same way as the reconstruction of Holland and Sardinia, and the subsequent proceedings of Talleyrand at Vienna would have been impossible. As it was, the Powers could only bind France by the first secret article to recognise that they had the ultimate decision. It was, indeed, already apparent to some that a Bourbon France could not be treated as a *quantité négligeable*.[1] If, however, the four Powers, as they hoped, could conclude their preliminary arrangements, they did not expect to have much trouble from Talleyrand at the Congress.

Section 13. The Preliminary Discussions in London. Diplomatic Preparations

The Tsar and the King of Prussia and their Ministers accepted the invitation of the Prince Regent to England, while Metternich represented the Emperor of Austria. It had been Castlereagh's intention to utilise this opportunity to complete the arrangements for the settlement of Europe.[2] Though this

---

[1] Münster to the Prince Regent, May 5, 1814, *Political Sketches*, p. 162. 'The existing Government of France cannot be excluded from taking any part in the arrangements made to settle the relations of the different Empires of Europe as it was formerly intended that Bonaparte's should be.'
[2] Castlereagh to Liverpool, Apr. 13, 1814; 'That the three great monarchs... proceeding there accompanied by their respective Ministers, our conferences might be continued in London and all essential points arranged for the ratification of Congress.' *Correspondence*, IX, 460.

E

expectation was not fulfilled, a very profound effect was produced by this visit on the political situation. The attitude which Castlereagh had adopted in France towards the Powers by no means represented the opinions of the Cabinet. Both the Prince Regent and the Prime Minister were at this time well disposed towards Alexander, and they distrusted Austria, and especially her Foreign Minister.[1]

Had the Tsar played his cards well, he might have made the position of Castlereagh an exceedingly difficult one. As events fell out, however, he permanently lost the friendship, not only of the Prince Regent, but also of the Tory Ministry. The Tsar's sister, the Grand Duchess Catharine, with whom his relations were of the most intimate kind, had preceded him to London. Despite the entreaties and protests of the Russian Ambassador and his wife, she flouted all social conventions, and, what was even worse, cultivated the Whigs rather than the Tories.[2] She even threatened to visit the unhappy Princess of Wales, with whom the Prince Regent had now publicly broken off relations, while to her influence on the Princess Charlotte was later ascribed the latter's refusal to marry the Prince of Orange. These strange proceedings were thoroughly approved of and closely imitated by Alexander. He won the plaudits of the mob and the half-hearted support of the Whigs at the cost of the hatred of the Prince Regent and the dislike of his Ministers. So far as his motives were political and not personal, he seems to have thought that he could best win support for his Polish schemes by an alliance with the leaders of the Opposition,[3] while the unpopularity of the Prince

[1] Merveldt to Metternich, Apr. 12, 1814, Vienna Archives.
[2] See the diary of Princess Lieven in the '*Correspondence de l'Empereur Alexandre avec sa Soeur*', edited by the Grand Duke Nicholas Michaelovitch.
[3] Merveldt to Metternich, July 9, 1814; 'Lord Castlereagh me parla du mouvement que se donnaient ici les Princes Tzartoriski et Radziwill pour engager des membres de l'opposition à porter devant le Parlement la question sur l'avenir de la Pologne.' Vienna Archives.

Regent and some of his Ministers may have given him the idea that the Tories would not remain long in power. If these were his motives, never was a greater political mistake committed. The Prince Regent and a Tory Ministry controlled British policy during Alexander's lifetime, and the effects of this visit were never eradicated. Metternich meanwhile paid assiduous court to the Prince Regent, and avoided all intercourse with the Opposition.[1]

This situation, while it brought Castlereagh and Metternich more closely together, prevented that settlement before the meeting of Congress which all the four Powers desired. The Polish and Saxon questions were, indeed, discussed by the four Ministers, but the Tsar showed himself even less conciliatory than at Paris. No formal consideration of these questions could, therefore, take place, and it was agreed to postpone it until the meeting at Vienna.[2] It had been originally intended that the Congress should meet at the beginning of August. But Castlereagh found that he could not get through his Parliamentary business in time; and, as Alexander now realised that the Congress was likely to last longer than had at first been anticipated, he wished first to visit Russia. This decision he announced only when on his way back to the Continent; and the Ministers had perforce to postpone the meeting till the end of September.[3]

The four Powers were also now faced with the fact that they had to meet Congress without having obtained a decision on the principal points in dispute. But they were still firm in their intention to decide these points by themselves. They resolved, therefore, that while the Powers who had signed the Treaty of Paris had the right to formulate a plan for the organisation of Congress, this must only be 'd'après le plan qui aura été arrêté

---

[1] He had instructed Merveldt to pursue a similar course of policy as early as Jan. 1814. Vienna Archives.
[2] Klinkowström, p. 393.   [3] Protocol of June 20, 1814, F.O. Continent 5.

entre les quatre cours'.[1] For this purpose the Ministers of the
four Courts were to meet at Vienna some little time before the
rest of Congress assembled. Alexander was somewhat sus-
picious of this last step, and only agreed to it on condition that
nothing was to be definitely decided before he appeared on the
scene.[2] The four Powers also agreed that no action should be
taken in the countries which they provisionally occupied
except in so far as their fate had already been definitely decided
by treaty.[3] This was a point of great importance. Russian troops
held all Poland and Saxony, as well as Holstein and other places
in the north, while Prussia was in possession of the territories
on the left bank of the Rhine and Mainz. The temptation to
produce a *fait accompli* was, therefore, considerable. Lastly, in
order that there might be no danger from France or other
disturbing elements, the four Powers agreed that each should
maintain at least 75,000 troops on a war footing until the new
order should be finally consummated.[4] This was almost
superfluous, for none of the Continental Powers had the
slightest intention of disarming so long as their territories were
undefined.

The only specific question which made any progress in the
London Conferences was that of the incorporation of the Low
Countries in Holland. The principles on which the new State
was to be governed were submitted to the Conference by
the Sovereign Prince and approved by the Allies; and the
provisional administration of the Belgian provinces was

[1] 'Points de délibération' endorsed Conference of June 16, F.O. Continent
5. These protocols, hitherto unpublished, are the only direct evidence of
these meetings, and historians have been puzzled. It is probable, however,
that, as the meetings were mainly informal, no others exist except those
concerning Belgium and the maintenance of the Allied armies, which have
long been known.
[2] 'Déclaration au protocole du 10/22 Juin', F.O. Continent 5. Nesselrode
to Alexander, June 12/24, 1814, Petrograd Archives.
[3] Protocol of the Conference of June 20, 1814, F.O. Continent 5.
[4] 'Convention supplémentaire' of June 29, 1814, D'Angeberg, 183.

transferred from the Austrians to its new ruler.[1] The frontiers of Holland beyond the Meuse could not, however, yet be decided, since they depended on the other arrangements; and the recognition of the new State was deferred until the Congress.

In the interval between the London Conferences and the Congress the activities of the Ministers of the Great Powers were necessarily absorbed to a considerable extent by domestic affairs, but they were also engaged in endeavouring to produce situations favourable to their own plans for the Congress. Thus Metternich attempted to strengthen in every way the coalition he was endeavouring to build up against Alexander. At a meeting in London, Münster and Hardenberg had attempted to settle the vexed questions of Luxemburg and Mainz, while Metternich had discussed with the Prussian Minister the constitution of the German Confederation.[2] On his return to Vienna he renewed his negotiations with Hardenberg; and, despite the fact that he found a strong party, headed by Stadion and Schwarzenberg, working against him, persisted in his offer of Saxony if Prussia would join him wholeheartedly in opposition to Alexander. Now was the time, he urged on Hardenberg, to undermine the influence which Alexander had acquired over the Prussian King. He also sent an emissary to Russia to ascertain how far opposition to the Tsar's plans could be discerned there.[3] In all these negotiations

---

[1] Protocol of June 14, D'Angeberg, 182. The question of the Dutch colonies was finally settled by a Convention of Aug. 13 between the Netherlands and Great Britain, by which the latter retained the Cape of Good Hope and some minor possessions, but returned the Dutch East Indies. A sum of two millions sterling was also paid to the Dutch to create fortifications on the French frontier; D'Angeberg, 209. See the paper on Holland in this series (No. 37); also that on Indemnities (No. 159).

[2] Memorandum of Hardenberg and Münster, June 15, 1814, F.O. Continent 5.

[3] Fournier, *Zur Vorgeschichte des Wiener Kongresses, Historische Studien und Skizzen*, II, p. 304.

he had a considerable measure of success, but an attempt to bring them to a conclusion by a preliminary meeting of the four Ministers at Baden was a failure.[1]

Nor was Castlereagh idle during this time. Much trouble was caused by the refusal of the Norwegians to accept Swedish rule; and a British fleet had to blockade their coasts. Eventually this matter was settled; and Prussia also signed a treaty with Denmark, by which the latter was promised Swedish Pomerania. The larger question was also not neglected. Castlereagh called Hardenberg's attention to Alexander's organisation of the Polish Army, and warned him to watch the activities of Russian troops in the north. In his reply the Prussian Minister stated that he hoped that Alexander was going to give way, as Metternich professed to believe; and he explained his own plans for the reconstruction of Europe. That Prussia would receive the whole of Saxony was, of course, assumed; but he also showed great jealousy of Austria's connections with Bavaria, and suggested that the two Great German Powers should partition the left bank of the Rhine between them.[2] This correspondence revealed how much there was still dividing Austria and Prussia. Nevertheless, Castlereagh saw in their union the sole hope of checking Russian aggrandisement.

Meanwhile, Talleyrand was drawing up his instructions for the Congress. This brilliant and deservedly famous document based the settlement of Europe on the principle of legitimacy, which would restore Saxony and Naples to their old rulers, and hoped to effect France's entrance into the European directorate by insisting on the rights of the smaller Powers. But Talleyrand was also seeking other means by which he might make his presence felt at the approaching reunion, while none

[1] Fournier, *Die Geheimpolizei auf dem Wiener Kongress*, p. 116.
[2] Castlereagh to Hardenberg, Aug. 8, 1814; Hardenberg to Castlereagh, Aug. 27, 1814; F.O. Continent Archives 20.

of the Great Powers was unconscious of the fact that France was a possible ally, should all other resources fail to settle the difficulties between them. Alexander was endeavouring to conclude a marriage between his sister Anne and the Duc de Berri, but he failed to conciliate Louis XVIII. Metternich had visited Paris on his way to Vienna, but he had adopted an attitude of precaution that had alarmed Talleyrand and his master.[1] It was to England that Talleyrand looked.

When, therefore, Castlereagh took the precaution of communicating the convention of June 29 to Talleyrand, and explaining the reasons for the postponement of the opening of the Congress, he was met with an eager request that France and England should act together at Vienna as the only two disinterested Powers. Talleyrand, who was greatly alarmed at the news that preliminary meetings would be held at Vienna previous to his arrival, opened his mind on the questions of Poland and Italy. He cleverly did not lay too much stress on the project of the dethronement of Murat, which his colleagues were now loudly advocating, and endeavoured to bring forward points in which he believed Castlereagh's views would coincide with his own. The negotiation culminated in an urgent request for Castlereagh to visit Paris on his way to Vienna.[2]

The advantages of Talleyrand's support were fully realised at London. Castlereagh had been rather uneasy from the first at the position in which the Coalition had placed France. But he was no more prepared than any other Minister of the four Powers to go back on his engagements and admit France as an equal party to their discussion. While, therefore, he received Talleyrand's overture cordially, he immediately made it clear

[1] Sir Charles Stuart to Castlereagh, July 4, 1814, F.O. France 97.
[2] Castlereagh to Sir Charles Stuart, July 4, 1814; Stuart to Castlereagh, July 28; F.O. France 96 and 97. Later letters in *W.S.D.*, IX, 180-86. Wellington to Castlereagh, Aug. 18, 1814. *Correspondence*, X, 94.

that he would only consent to meet him on the understanding that the Alliance of the four Powers remained intact. But he agreed to visit Paris on his way to Vienna, and in two long interviews with Louis XVIII and his Minister he went over with them the whole of the questions at issue. Their support on the Polish question was freely offered; and Castlereagh had rather to repress than encourage their desire to co-operate with Great Britain. He succeeded in placing the preliminary meetings at Vienna in such a light that Talleyrand could offer no objections. He allowed Castlereagh to be the agent to express the views of the French Government until his own arrival. This important interview placed Castlereagh at the outset in a position towards France somewhat different from that which his Allies had adopted, though he had not committed himself to any definite line of action.[1] The special influence which he had thus acquired he was to use with advantage at the Congress in the course of the next few months.

[1] Castlereagh to Liverpool, Sept. 3, 1814, F.O. Continent 7; *Sbornik of the Russian Imperial Historical Society*, vol. CXII; *cf.* Alison Phillips, *The Confederation of Europe*, p. 96.

Part Two

THE ORGANISATION OF THE CONGRESS OF VIENNA

Section 14. The Problems and Personalities of the Congress

When the Powers, by Article XXXII of the Treaty of Paris, agreed that the settlement of European affairs should be regulated at a Congress, they struck the imagination of all Europe. The peoples did not know of the first secret article by which the Allied Powers intended to keep affairs in their own hands. They had vague historical recollections which carried them back to the treaties of Westphalia, and they looked on the Congress as a constituent body of Europe which should settle on lofty principles of justice and equity the great problems resulting from twenty years of war. The dispossessed princes and potentates, who had been submerged in the great flood of the Revolution and Empire, saw, indeed, in the Congress an assembly which would restore their stolen 'rights', while the Governments of the smaller States looked to Europe to round off their possessions by giving them long-coveted cities and counties. But the peoples as a whole expected something more. Many of the Germans, whose nationality had been awakened by the victorious struggle against Napoleon, were eager to obtain new institutions by which they would be able to express their new ideals. Similar aspirations, though not so strong and widespread, were also to be found in Italy. In England it was hoped that the humanitarian movement for the abolition of the slave trade would be strengthened by the approval of all Europe. In all countries there was a feeling, if vague and ill-defined, that some means should be found to prevent the recurrence of those evils from which the existing generation had so grievously suffered.

It has been seen how little the statesmen who were directing the affairs of Europe were occupied with these matters. For all of them, except for Talleyrand, who was vainly attempting to place himself at their side, the Congress was little more than a convenient assembly of diplomatists which would make it easier for them to consign to paper the agreements they would ultimately conclude. They had put forward the word 'Congress' imprudently, without reflecting upon all the results that the word implied. It had been an expedient to postpone, and perhaps to solve, their difficulties. But the invitation had been given and accepted by all the States of Europe; and the Great Powers were committed to admit them in some way to their councils. The result was that there came to Vienna an enormous number of plenipotentiaries imbued with vague aspirations and ill-considered designs, only to find no principle which should govern their procedure and no machinery by which they could be made into a coherent body. No appreciable difference would have been made in the final settlement at Vienna if the large majority of the plenipotentiaries had never appeared there at all. They merely acted as a picturesque and expensive background to the real Congress of Vienna. The stages by which this result was brought about will be described in the succeeding sections, but the problem of the Congress and the representatives who took part in it may be briefly indicated here in order to render what follows more intelligible.

The Congress had been called into being by the Treaties of Paris, and its programme was, in a sense, provided at the same time. Certain matters had been indicated for settlement in the public and secret articles of the treaties, such as the extension of the Kingdom of the Netherlands, the creation of a

German Federation, and a Constitution for Switzerland and the more general topics of the navigation of international rivers and the abolition of the slave trade; but the most important subjects of the Congress, the territorial changes to be made in Poland and Germany, which affected 32,000,000 inhabitants, had not even been mentioned. The wording of Article XXXII of the Paris Treaties allowed any subject to be brought forward which could be considered necessary to complete the few and vague specific references that had been given.

The primary task of the Congress was the redistribution of the conquered territories. In effecting this redistribution it was necessary to take into account not only the stipulations of the Treaties of Paris but also the treaties made in 1813 by the three Eastern Powers, both among themselves and with the minor States. As has been seen, these Powers had so far exhausted in vain every expedient to come to a decision. The principal stumbling-block had been the question of Poland. On this depended the fate of Saxony; and on the disposal of Saxony depended all the other arrangements in Germany, so that the frontier of almost every German State was likely to be affected. In Italy the frontier of the Austrian dominions and the incorporation of Genoa in Sardinia were already determined. But the fate of the territory that lay between the Papal dominions and Austria, including the three Legations, was still uncertain, while the Bourbon Powers had determined never to recognise Murat, and the Great Powers were already repenting of the treaty which, with their consent, Austria had signed with him. The fate of the Ionian Isles, then in British occupation, depended ultimately on the problem of Sicily. In the north, while the Norwegians had submitted at last to come under Swedish rule, there were still complicated questions to be settled in which Sweden, Hanover, and Prussia were interested. The boundaries of the new Kingdom of Holland had also to be defined. When it is remembered that constitutions had also to be given to Germany and Switzerland—problems in which the history of centuries was accumulated—it can be seen that the time available for the treatment of more general questions, such as those of the international rivers and of the abolition of the slave trade, was not likely to be great, while only great pressure of public opinion could be expected to make the statesmen consider seriously such problems as the construction of an international tribunal, the possibilities of general disarmament, or the creation of representative institutions.

By the Treaties of Paris all the States of Europe which had participated in the war had the right to send plenipotentiaries to Vienna; and every State availed itself of the privilege. The four Great Powers were represented by the same Ministers who had so long transacted business together, but to each were added new assistants, who in some cases played a considerable part in affairs. Thus Castlereagh took with him his half-brother, Lord Stewart, together with Lord Cathcart, both of whom had represented him on the Continent since 1813. To these he added Lord Clancarty, recently his Minister at The Hague, and the holder of minor offices in the Ministry, an indefatigable and tenacious diplomatist, who was to be one of the real workers of the Congress. These three were all plenipotentiaries, but the first two gave him little assistance, and Lord Stewart was to be the laughing-stock of Vienna. Wellington relieved Castlereagh in the middle of February. He was no diplomatist, but his courage and military reputation were used to advantage when Napoleon's escape was announced. Clancarty was in charge after Wellington's departure at the end of March. Castlereagh's technical staff included Edward Cooke, the Under-Secretary of State, an experienced official, who got into close touch with Metternich's secretaries. His mordant letters to the Prime Minister gave great satisfaction. Castlereagh also took with him Planta, his private secretary, and other officials, while Stratford Canning, the Minister of Berne, was summoned to assist at the Conferences on the Swiss Question. For military opinions Castlereagh relied almost entirely on Wellington, when he was not content to use those supplied by the Prussian and Austrian General Staffs. The British personnel was far too small in number for the vast amount of business to be got through; the mere copying of despatches was at times overwhelming. But it was well organised and disciplined, at any rate during Castlereagh's own stay at Vienna.

Hardenberg and Humboldt represented Prussia, whose King was forced to take a considerable share in events. They had a very efficient staff which included real experts, among them Hoffmann, one of the best statisticians in Europe, who was to prove very useful. They produced more memoranda than any other Power, but their diplomacy did not prove equal to their technical ability. This last fact was partly the fault of the General Staff, who constantly interfered.

Alexander surrounded himself with Ministers who were almost entirely non-Russian. Nesselrode was still Foreign Secretary, but he was entirely out of favour during the critical period of the Congress; Razumoffski and Stackelberg, the other two plenipotentiaries, were colourless persons. Czartoryski continued to advise the Tsar on Poland, and wrote most of his memoranda concerning that country; Capo d'Istria had great influence on Alexander's general policy; Stein, though somewhat disillusioned, still advised on German affairs: Laharpe controlled the attitude of Russia in the discussions on his native country; while the Corsican Pozzo di Borgo was summoned from Paris to give advice, which was not, however, well received. The Tsar himself exercised complete control, and chose the instruments of his policy as the situation of the moment dictated.

As for Austria, Metternich was in his own capital, and had

a large and, on the whole, very efficient diplomatic machine at his disposal. Wessenberg, the second Austrian plenipotentiary, was a good diplomatist, and supplied the industry which his chief lacked. Hudelist, a permanent official, and Gentz, one of the most facile writers in Europe, who was just beginning to gain his chief's confidence, inspired much of Metternich's policy, and helped to draft his memoranda. Throughout there was a party, of which Stadion and Schwarzenberg became the leaders, which objected to his policy, and did their best to discredit him.

France was represented by Talleyrand, who brought with him as plenipotentiaries three rather mediocre diplomatists, of whom the most important, Dalberg, though hard-working, was self-opinionated and very indiscreet. His principal assistant was La Besnardière, a permanent official of wide experience and a brilliant writer, who exercised great influence until the return of Napoleon.

Of the three other signatories of the Paris Treaties, Spain was represented by Labrador, who most ineptly tried to imitate Talleyrand; Portugal principally by Palmella, whose Court in Brazil was so distant that he was not able to play much part; and Sweden by Lövenheilm, who passively looked on at the struggles in which his master, Bernadotte, now professed to take no interest.

Of the minor Powers, only a few of the plenipotentiaries exercised much influence. Münster, who represented the Prince Regent as ruler of Hanover, was also at times used by Castlereagh for other purposes. Holland was represented by Van Spaen and von Gagen, who resented keenly, without being able to alter, the secondary part which they were forced to play. Their policy was settled in the last event by England; and Clancarty corresponded with the Dutch Sovereign throughout the Congress. Field-Marshal Wrede arrogantly defended Bavaria's interests. Both Murat and Ferdinand of

Sicily had representatives at the Congress. All the minor States of Italy and Germany, as well as a large number of German princes and counts of the Empire who had been deprived of their sovereign rights during the upheaval in Germany, sent representatives. There were also present a large number of royalties, including the Kings of Bavaria, Württemberg, and Denmark, and many smaller monarchs. The Pope was represented by Cardinal Consalvi, who played a singularly narrow rôle, in spite of his undoubted ability; the Sultan by Mavrogeni, his *chargé d'affaires* at Vienna, a Greek by nationality.

Added to these were representatives of many special interests, some as imposing as the German Catholics or as influential as the German Jews, others of little importance, amongst them the Order of St. John, which still had hopes of compensation for Malta. Even the deposed King of Sweden had Sir Sidney Smith, the defender of Acre, to uphold his cause.

When it is remembered that a large number of the sovereigns and diplomatists brought with them their wives and other female relations, the extraordinary spectacle which Vienna presented can be imagined. It attracted, naturally, a large number of visitors, who seem to have been admitted without even the excuse of business; and the presence of the courtiers and rich of all countries added to the difficulties of accommodation and supply which were throughout harassing to all concerned.

Section 15. *First Discussions as to the Organisation of the Congress*

By September 13, 1814, the Ministers of the four Powers had reached Vienna; and discussions were immediately begun touching the organisation of the Congress. They were agreed in substance as to the necessity of keeping the control of the decisions in their own hands, but the delicate question as to how the determination was to be communicated to the other plenipotentiaries had now to be faced. There were no precedents of much value as to how the Congress should be constituted. The Congress had not met to make a treaty of peace; and to define the status and powers of the vast number of plenipotentiaries who wished to take part was not easy, even if there had been anything like a consensus of opinion on the subjects to be discussed.

The informal meetings, in which Castlereagh and Metternich consulted first Nesselrode and then Hardenberg and Humboldt, began on September 15; and these led to four Conferences, at which these Ministers met in order to give their discussions a shape in which they could be communicated to the rest of Europe. It was universally agreed 'that the conduct of the business must practically rest with the leading Powers'; but in defining the 'leading Powers' an entirely new distinction was now introduced for the first time. 'We are agreed,' wrote Castlereagh, 'that the effective Cabinet should not be carried beyond the six Powers of the first order.'[1] Thus the final directing Cabinet was to be based, not on the Treaty of Paris or on any other public document, but on a distinction between 'great' and 'small' Powers. The four Allies, together with France and Spain, were to be considered the Great Powers. The first expression of the idea of the Great Powers, with rights as such, distinct from any derived from treaties, may perhaps be dated from this meeting.

But this was to be merely the formal directing Cabinet. The Allies deemed it necessary to preserve the 'initiation' in their own hands and by 'initiation' they really meant 'decision'. They based their claim to effect this on the first secret article of the Paris Treaty, which, according to their interpretation, gave them the right to come to a preliminary decision, not only on

---

[1] Castlereagh to Liverpool, Sept. 19, 24, 1814. F.O. Continent 7.

the subjects mentioned in the articles attached to the Paris Treaty, but also on the disposition of the whole of the conquered territories. This principle was definitely stated in a protocol of September 22, which had been drawn up by the Prussians. Its object was to prevent France from mingling in the discussions and using the differences of the Allies to further her own designs. The blunt way in which this was stated was considered by Castlereagh, fresh from his conciliatory interview with Talleyrand, 'to be rather repulsive against France and a little more conclusive in its expressions' than he quite liked. He accordingly added a separate declaration to the protocol,[1] which asserted that the discussion with France or Spain was to be conducted as towards friendly and not hostile Powers. He further reserved to himself the right to dissent from any decision of the 'four' with which he could not agree.

There was then to be a sham directing Committee of the six Powers; with a real inner Committee of the four Powers: but what of the Congress as a whole. How was it to be assembled, and how was its business to be conducted? How was the decision of the Great Powers to keep matters in their own hands to be communicated to the other States without provoking a united protest? On this point none of the Ministers had at the outset any very definite plan; and the record[2] which Castlereagh despatched to London shows how diffidently they approached the subject and how their ideas changed in the course of the discussion. The first proposal was to constitute the Congress by summoning the plenipotentiaries, and then getting them to appoint a Committee to prepare a scheme for their consideration. But, as Castlereagh pointed out, this would have immediately involved the Powers

---

[1] Protocols of Sept. 22, *British and Foreign State Papers*, II, p. 554-5.
[2] See Appendices I, II, III, IV, V, VI. There is an account by Gentz, but it merely indicates the difficulties. The protocols and some of the letters are published in D'Angeberg and *B. and F.S.P.*, vol. II. Some of the points are still obscure, and it is not easy to assign to some of the memoranda in the F.O. Records their exact place in the discussions.

F

'without previous concert in all the preliminary questions of difficulty—*viz.*, what Powers shall be admitted to sit and deliberate and what only to petition and negotiate, what are to be the functions and attributions of the Congress, and by what mode they are to act and conclude'.

It was at once abandoned, therefore, and a scheme substituted by which the six Powers should simply assume control, without any authorisation, and announce that the preliminary decisions must first be made by themselves, other Powers being consulted when the necessity arose. This point of view was strongly urged by the Prussians in a memorandum written by Humboldt, which, after dividing the subjects to be discussed by various Committees in a manner which in effect would have given control to the four, suggested that these Committees should first draw up in treaty form their decisions, that these decisions should then be discussed by the formal directing Committee of the six, and, lastly, communicated by it to the Powers whom it concerned. This procedure he proposed to set in motion at once, without any preliminary meeting.[1]

To Castlereagh, however, though he agreed with the substance of these proposals, this appeared too open a disclosure of the intentions of the four. He preferred, if possible, to obtain the sanction of the rest of Europe to the ascendency of the Great Powers. Accordingly, he suggested a scheme by which, at a preliminary meeting of all the plenipotentiaries, they might be induced to allow the six Great Powers to manage affairs for them. In two papers he worked out the whole plan in great detail.[2] It is characteristic of his policy that he proposed to get the scheme through by making it as palatable as possible to the smaller Powers and using the influence of the Great Powers to manage the voting. In this way he thought that the six Powers would be accepted as a formal directing Committee almost universally, and that any opposition would be easily

[1] See Appendix IV.   [2] See the papers in Appendix III, p. 152.

overcome. It was impossible to be certain, however, how the Conference of Plenipotentiaries would act; and the question of the exact status of the Neopolitan and Saxon plenipotentiaries would, in a sense, be raised merely by summoning the plenipotentiaries together. These difficulties were insisted upon in a second memorandum drawn up by Humboldt, which, with true Prussian disregard of nice susceptibilities, proposed to issue a declaration that the six Powers would direct the business of the Congress, and would summon other Powers to such discussions as they thought fit.[1] Castlereagh thought that this idea was objectionable, as

> 'it too broadly and ostensibly assumed the right to do what may be generally acquiesced in if not offensively announced, but which the secondary Powers may protest against, if recorded to their humiliation in the face of Europe'.

He had not, however, sufficient confidence in his own proposal of an opening meeting to press it further in the face of this opposition.

The question was thus left open until the plenipotentiaries of France and Spain arrived, with the intention that the Congress should simply be postponed until there had been 'confidential intercourse' between the plenipotentiaries. Neither Castlereagh nor the others quite realised the opportunity which their indecision would give to Talleyrand. Castlereagh had loyally endeavoured to arrange a working agreement on the lines he had laid down at Paris, but he found that the other three Courts were strongly against 'admitting France either to arbitrate between them or to assume any leading influence in the arrangements consequent upon the peace'. The final result

[1] 'Proposal of Baron Humboldt to publish a Declaration.' See Appendix V, p. 162. He also ingeniously suggested that the Declaration might be issued by each of the six Powers individually in its own name on behalf of the others. By this means one Power could communicate it to plenipotentiaries whom the others did not wish to recognise without committing the rest. See Appendix VI.

was that the four Powers signed a protocol which reserved the settlement of the territorial questions to themselves. Their decisions were to be first communicated to France and Spain, and then to the Congress as a whole. The arrangements for the formal Congress were to be discussed between the six Powers. A Special Committee of the five principal German Powers was to be set up to draft the scheme for a German Federation.[1]

Talleyrand arrived on the evening of the 23rd; and on the 30th, together with Labrador, the Spanish plenipotentiary, he was invited to a Conference in order that these decisions might be communicated to him in as palatable a fashion as possible. The scene described by himself in much detail has become memorable in history, and has perhaps had too much importance attached to it. Talleyrand, supported by Labrador, used all his diplomatic arts of persuasion, insinuation, and intimidation to claim from the first a position of full equality with the four Powers, and he endeavoured to appeal from their authority to the Congress as a whole.[2] In this he was not successful, but he was able to disarrange the plans the four Powers had made. A protocol was shown him, which, though less strongly worded than those which recorded the decisions of the 22nd, of which he was not to know till much later, yet was sufficiently inept in that it emphasised the word 'Allies'.[3] Talleyrand refused even to consider this document. It was therefore withdrawn, and a *Projet* of Declaration for the opening of the Congress was submitted to him, which simply left the general direction of affairs in the hands of the six Powers. This was reserved for

[1] 'Projet des 4 Cours sur les Formes du Congrès,' Sept. 22, 1814, *B. and F.S.P.*, I, 556.

[2] Pallain, *Correspondance de Talleyrand pendant le Congrès de Vienne*, p. 10; *Dépêches Inédtes*, I, 108.

[3] The exact form is not known except from his own account. Talleyrand did not know of the protocols of the 22nd until March, 1815. See Pallain, p. 337.

consideration; and the meeting broke up after Talleyrand had expatiated on the responsibilities of Constitutional Powers such as England and France, and intimated that he saw no reason why the Congress should not at once assemble. That evening he addressed a formal reply to the Ministers of the four Courts,[1] in which he claimed that the Congress must meet at once, and, while he admitted that a directing Council was necessary, suggested that the only legal body that could act as a preliminary Committee was one consisting of the eight Powers which had signed the Treaties of Paris, which would have added Portugal and Sweden to the six. For it was by the Paris Treaties that the Congress itself had come into being; and the position of the convening Powers must be immediately made regular by the approval of the whole Congress.

The four Ministers met on the morning of October 1 to consider their reply.[2] The formal character which Talleyrand had given to his answer was viewed with great disfavour, as they had intended their overtures to be regarded as unofficial and confidential. They decided to abandon the idea of the six Powers altogether, since it rested on no documentary ground, and to accept Talleyrand's proposition of the eight Powers, signatories of the Paris Treaties, as the formal directing Committee.[3] They adhered, however, to their determination that the Congress itself should not meet until the directing Powers had determined its procedure and method of business. It was also decided that this reply should be submitted to Talleyrand

---

[1] *B. and F.S.P.*, II, 559.

[2] 'Conférence du 2 Octobre entre les Ministres d'Autriche, de Prusse, de Russie et d'Angleterre' bears the note; 'Il a été décidé que cette pièce sera simplement conservée comme mémorandum de la susdite Conférence', F.O. Continent 7.

[3] Palmella, the Portuguese plenipotentiary, had already sent, in collusion with Talleyrand, a protest against his exclusion from the first meeting. Pamella to Castlereagh, Sept. 30, 1814, F.O. Continent 7. Lövenheilm, the Swedish representative, contented himself with formally announcing his arrival. Fournier, *Die Geheimpolizei*, etc., p. 221.

orally, and that no formal answer should be sent if it could be avoided. Talleyrand was accordingly told their opinion at a social meeting in the evening.[1] He discerned the embarrassment of the 'four', and endeavoured in every way to increase it. He allowed the fact of the controversy to become known; and a meeting of the smaller German Powers was held to support him. Fortified by assurances of support, he formally rejected the *projet de déclaration* originally drawn up by Castlereagh, which was submitted to him as an alternative procedure,[2] and in a letter[3] to Castlereagh of October 5 he again insisted on the necessity of the Congress being at once constituted.

An informal Conference between Talleyrand and the Ministers of the four Powers followed on October 5, in which the former was asked to withdraw his note. He refused; but, after some discussion with Metternich, consented that the Congress should be postponed, provided, however, that it was for a definite period only, and that a *règle* of his own composition, in accordance with which the plenipotentiaries were to meet, should be at once announced.[4] This *règle*, which was expressly designed to admit Saxony and exclude Neapolitan plenipotentiaries, broke up the meeting, Castlereagh, as they departed, in vain endeavouring to secure Talleyrand's acquiescence to his views. But, if Talleyrand had scored a formal victory in substituting the 'eight' for the 'six' he had already

---

[1] Talleyrand, *Mémoires*, II, 328.   [2] *B. and F.S.P.*, II, 560.   [3] *Ibid.*, II, 561.
[4] Talleyrand, *Mémoires*, II, 339. The *règle*, which was not, of course, invented at the moment, but drawn from his instructions, was as follows; 'Que tout Prince ayant sur des États qui ont été engagés dans la dernière guerre un droit de souveraineté qui a été universellement reconnu, qu'il n'a point cédé, et qui n'est reconnu à aucun autre, peut, de même que tout État que la dernière guerre a trouvé libre, qui y a été engagé et qui est actuellement libre, avoir des plénipotentiaires au Congrès; qu'aucun autre Prince ou État ne le peut pas.' F.O. Continent 7. This, as a marginal note on the F.O. copy points out, 'would have excluded Naples, but admitted Saxony; considered, therefore, by Prussia as particularly hostile to her interests'. See Alison Phillips. *op. cit.*, p. 102.

given way on the point that the Congress must be postponed; and his *règle*, which opened up the Neapolitan question at the very outset, was premature and ill-advised. Yet without some such rule even a meeting of the plenipotentiaries was impossible since it was imperative to decide who had a right to be summoned.[1] Hardenberg was clearly on unshakeable ground when he said that no plan could be considered which would give the minor princelings the right to intervene in the general arrangements of Europe.

The four Powers, therefore, stuck to their idea; and Gentz was set to the task of preparing another declaration. A further Conference did not take place till October 8th, Talleyrand being flattered by Metternich[2] in a special interview before the meeting with some general observations on the Polish-Saxon questions. At this Conference the four Powers unanimously decided to adopt Gentz's declaration, which merely announced the postponement of the Congress till November 1, in order to give time for reflection. Talleyrand this time gave his consent. He covered his defeat by insisting on the addition of a sentence that the Congress would conform 'aux principes du droit public'. According to Talleyrand's own account, a tumult was produced at this simple proposal, which the Prussians took as deliberately aimed at themselves. But the addition of the words to the declaration in no way altered its character. While Talleyrand, therefore, had prevented any formal recognition of the rights of the four Powers of the Committee of Six, he had secured little else. The opening of the Congress was postponed; and, if he could not appeal to Congress he was helpless against the four, so long as they were united in their decision to keep control. But the real business of the Congress was already being carried on in informal meetings of the Ministers of the four Powers and private correspondence

---

[1] Castlereagh to Liverpool, Oct. 9, 1814, F.O. Continent 7.
[2] Talleyrand, *Mémoires*, II, 342.

between them and Alexander; from these momentous discussions Talleyrand was entirely excluded.

Section 16. The Second Attempt to Constitute Congress. Further Postponement

This situation continued throughout the whole of October. The four Courts engaged in violent controversy over the Saxon-Polish question; but the only formal Conferences which took place were those assembled to consider the question of the German Constitution. A committee of the five principal German Powers (Austria, Prussia, Bavaria, Hanover, and Württemberg) met on October 14 for this purpose, entirely in defiance of Talleyrand's ideas, and without any authority from the Congress, the eight, or any other body. It based its existence simply on the Treaty of Paris, and itself decided who should be members of it.[1] At the end of the month the question of the opening of the Congress had necessarily to be further considered. The energies of the four Powers had been absorbed in the Polish-Saxon controversy, and they appear to have devoted little time to considering the question of organisation. Talleyrand, excluded from all participation in these critical debates, was able to prepare his own plans at leisure. He had already, however, receded somewhat from his first uncompromising attitude; and both Castlereagh and Metternich, by keeping him to some extent informed as to their disputes, had made him still more conciliatory. The threat of an appeal to the Congress had even been contemplated by Castlereagh as a means of intimidating the Emperor of Russia, though he does not seem to have had any clear idea of what he meant by the term,[2]

---

[1] 'Premier Protocole du Comité institué pour les affaires d'Allemagne, Séance du 14 Octobre, 1814', D'Angeberg, p. 289.

[2] He proposed to Austria and Prussia in the *Memorandum on Poland*, dated Oct. 24, 1814, that copies of the correspondence concerning Poland should, if necessary, 'be laid before Congress', and 'that the several Powers of Europe should be invited . . . to declare to the Emperor of Russia to what extent and

while Metternich did actually use the threat in a conversation with Alexander, who simply replied that he did not care for the Congress.[1] But the two Ministers do not seem to have done more than see what the effects of the threat would be.

It was the full Committee of the eight which met on October 30 to consider once more the constitution of Congress; and Talleyrand was further flattered by a request from Castlereagh to submit a plan to this body.[2] At this meeting and a subsequent one on the next day Talleyrand therefore brought forward a new scheme. He proposed as a directing Committee for the Congress a *Commission générale*, comprised of representatives of all the sovereign heads (including the Pope). By this General Committee four sub-Committees were to be nominated to discuss the questions of Poland, Saxony, Switzerland, and Italy. The sub-Committees were to report to the General Committee, which in its turn was to report to the Congress. Plenipotentiaries (such as those of Murat or the King of Saxony), whose position might be challenged, were to be present at discussions, but not to vote. Meanwhile, the full powers of all plenipotentiaries were to be examined, with a view to the whole Congress being summoned to consider the work of the *Commission générale*.[3] But, despite their dissensions, the four were no more ready than before to submit. The

upon what conditions Europe in Congress can or cannot admit His Imperial Majesty's pretensions to an aggrandisement in Poland'. 'It is desirable,' he added, 'that the Emperor should be made distinctly to understand that.... it would rest with the Powers in Congress assembled to decide upon the measures which should be called for by so alarming an infraction of treaties.' F.O. Continent 7. D'Angeberg, p. 291. French translation, with wrong date.

[1] Münster to the Prince Regent, Oct. 25, 1814, Hanover Archives; 'Il (Metternich) n'a réussi qu'à s'attirer une sortie des plus vives de la part de l'Empereur, qui l'a accusé de vouloir le menacer de l'appui d'un Congrès pour lequel il n'avoit aucun égard.'

[2] Pallain, p. 91.

[3] *B. and F.S.P.*, II, 563 ff.

difference between them and Talleyrand was, indeed, too great to be bridged by any scheme, however ingenious. Talleyrand postulated that the Congress as a whole should be the supreme Council of Europe, and really should decide the questions in dispute. The four Powers regarded it merely as a convenient assembly to facilitate their own decisions.[1]

The only step that was taken, therefore, was the appointment by lot of a Committee of three Powers to verify the full powers of the plenipotentiaries, while Metternich was formally elected president[2] of the Committee of Eight. Talleyrand's agreement, with scarcely a struggle, can only be explained by the fact that he was beginning himself to realise the hopelessness of his position, and hoped to gain more by an alliance with Castlereagh and Metternich than by maintaining his previous attitude. He passes over these decisions with few words in his letters to the King, for he could not claim to have played a *beau rôle*. Thus, though the plenipotentiaries hastened to send in their full powers, which were duly examined, there was no word of the opening of Congress; and at a meeting of the eight on November 18 it was postponed to an indefinite date.[3] That date was, of course, never reached, and the Congress of the whole body of plenipotentiaries never came into existence at all.

Meanwhile, the organisation for the transaction of business grew out of the necessities of the situation; and machinery was

---

[1] The situation was well described by Lövenheilm on November 5; 'La seule démarche à laquelle les plénipotentiaires russes, prussiens, anglais et autrichiens se soumettent vis-à-vis du Congrès est la connaissance qu'ils veulent donner à toute l'Europe de leurs arrangements respectifs. . . . Les plénipotentiaires français entendent le mot "Congrès" dans son acceptation ordinaire, . . . les Ministres des autre grandes puissances ne veulent point s'en tenir à cette notion connue mais le considérer simplement comme une réunion de toutes les puissances sur un même point pour faciliter leurs arrangements.' Fournier, *Die Geheimpolizei, etc.*, p. 278.

[2] *B. and F.S.P.*, II, 563.

[3] *Ibid.*, 570.

set up which derived its authority from no consistent p/
The Committee of Eight assumed without further auu..
tion the position of a formal directing Committee; the
Federal Constitution was continually discussed by the German
Committee, which also at times discussed the territorial
arrangements. The reunion of Sardinia and Genoa, already
decided on in principle at Paris, was ratified by the Committee
of Eight, the request of Talleyrand and Labrador to proceed
with the other Italian affairs being refused; and special Committees were formed on the nomination of the four Powers to
consider the affairs of Switzerland. But the real kernel of the
whole settlement, the Polish-Saxon question, which involved
also the whole territorial distribution of Germany, was discussed in no formal Committee at all, but merely by interviews
and the exchange of letters and memoranda between the
representatives of the four. The determination of the four to
keep these matters in their own hands persisted until they
found themselves on the verge of war, and neither Talleyrand nor anyone else could alter their decision. The only thing
that he had done was to prevent these meetings of the four Powers
from being officially recognised; but all knew that, if once an
agreement could be reached, their decisions must be ratified
by the rest of Europe. The reason why they allowed the matter
to drag on was because they had drifted into open opposition,
which grew daily more and more irreconcilable. The attention
of the principal statesmen was, in fact, directed so much to the
substance of the negotiations that the form had become a
secondary matter, and the ascendancy of the four was so great
that the plenipotentiaries of the other Powers had no business to
transact. Castlereagh did not even report on these changes in
organisation until November 21, when he was able to announce that all opposition was dying away, and that the
impossibility of assembling Congress and the gradual growth
of a suitable organisation had been submitted to, both by

Talleyrand and by the other plenipotentiaries.[1] Both Metternich and Castlereagh, despairing of overcoming the Prusso-Russian alliance, were indeed now beginning to treat Talleyrand with more confidence, with the result that the latter showed himself more and more accommodating in the matter of organisation. Conferences of the eight Powers were held on December 9, 10, and 14, at which, on the initiative of Talleyrand, Committees were set up on the question of the rank of diplomatic representatives (all the eight Powers having members) and on the navigation of international rivers, Austria, France, Great Britain, and Prussia being represented; while only the opposition of Spain and Portugal prevented a formal Committee from being also appointed to consider the abolition of the slave trade.[2]

Section 17. *The Constitution of the Committee of Five; the Real Congress*

This rapprochement between France and Great Britain and Austria was soon to receive more formal expression. Towards the end of December Castlereagh proposed to the other members of the four the formation of a Statistical Commission to ascertain the real numbers of the populations of the territories in dispute, and provide some basis of settlement.[3] It had not at first been his intention to include a French plenipotentiary on this Committee, which would have to play an important part in determining the territorial distribution; but, when Talleyrand made it an essential condition for the continuance of his support that France should be represented on it, both Castlereagh and Metternich acquiesced.[4]

---

[1] Castlereagh to Liverpool, Nov. 21, 1814, F.O. Continent 9.
[2] B. and F.S.P., II, 573, 578.
[3] Castlereagh to Liverpool, Dec. 24, 1814, F.O. Continent 9. See below, Section 21.
[4] Pallain, p. 200; W.S.D., IX, 503.

There shortly followed a complete change in the constitution of the Congress. Again it was the logic of events and not the deliberate planning of the statesmen that determined the forms by which they worked. On December 24 Alexander insisted on bringing to formal conferences the discussion on the Polish question, which had now lasted three months, and had reached a complete deadlock. The Committee of Four, therefore, which had hitherto only met in the most informal way, was now constituted as a formal conference.[1] At its first meeting Castlereagh and Metternich insisted that France should be represented.[2] The explosion that ensued and the signature of the Secret Treaty of January 3, 1815, are narrated in a subsequent section (see pp. 125-134).[3] But the result of the defeat of Prussian truculence was to turn the Committee of Four into a Committee of Five.[4] For over a week the issue hung in the balance; but eventually Prussia gave way, and at the last meeting on January 9 Castlereagh made a formal demand for the inclusion of France, which was agreed to by all the Four Powers.

Thus, at last, Talleyrand had won his way into the real directing Committee. This result had, however, been less due to any effort or intrigue on his part than to the fact that the four Powers had been unable to agree, and had, in fact, come to the verge of war. But Talleyrand, now that he was admitted to the inner Committee, abandoned all ideas of constituting a general Congress; and no more was heard of the rights of the small Powers. The result was that the formal Committee of Five, originally designed merely to settle the Saxon question, became the real directing Committee of the Congress. It at first settled, piece by piece, the territorial distribution of

---

[1] D'Angeberg, p. 1861.
[2] Castlereagh to Liverpool, Jan. 1, 1814, F.O. Continent 10.
[3] See Section 25.
[4] Protocol of Jan. 9, *B. and F.S.P.*, II, 597, 601.

Germany; and, when this was accomplished, it reviewed and adjusted the reports of the other Committees. In fact, it worked out the territorial details of the Treaty of Vienna, and the actual agreements were recorded in its protocols. The Committee of Eight only met nine times before the last Conferences to sign the Final Act, while in the same period the Committee of Five held forty-one meetings. The truth is, that at last the natural and normal organ of work had been found. The Committee of Five represented the force that governed Europe. Once the five Great Powers were really determined on settlement, this was the obvious means to bring it about. The proposal, therefore, which had been suggested in the early meetings of a Committee of the Great Powers directing the Congress, was finally brought about, though only by the admission of France to an equal place with the four and the recognition that Spain was not a Great Power.

The Committee of Five, then, is the 'real Congress of Vienna'.[1] Its first business was to arrange the compromises on the main territorial settlement which were concluded between January 7 and February 13. Castlereagh, who was determined not to leave Vienna while a subject was left open which was likely to lead to war amongst the Great Powers, took the lead in these transactions. Using the information provided for him by the Statistical Commission, by interview after interview with Sovereigns and Ministers, he gradually secured a distribution of the German and Polish territories, which all the three Powers interested were able to accept. These arrangements were then formally adopted in the Committee of Five, and recorded on its protocols; and so rapidly was the work done that on February 8 a Drafting Committee was appointed by the Five to work out the plan of a general treaty. Though

---

[1] So described by Humboldt in his 'Systematic Description of the Proceedings of the Congress of Vienna', June 15, 1815, quoted in Treitschke, *op. cit.*, II, 72.

some thorny questions, such as the territorial arrangements between Austria and Bavaria, were to occupy the Committee for a considerable time, the main difficulties were now over. Except in one particular, the Committee of Five, after Castlereagh's departure, was dealing with questions of which the principle had been settled, and which were, therefore, susceptible of treatment by minor diplomatic functionaries; and officials so skilled as Gentz and La Besnardière soon turned the complicated discussions as to territory, servitudes, boundaries, royal and feudal domains, debts and commercial interests, into articles which are attached to the protocols, and thus made ready for a treaty. The exception was the situation created by the return of Napoleon. For the Committee of Five also acted as a political and military Committee to direct the coalition against France, and on its protocols were recorded the decisions necessary to meet the new danger.

Section 18. The Functions of the Committee of Eight and of the German Committee

Though the Committee of Five became the centre of the Congress, the Committee of Eight still existed, and met on several occasions. It was retained as an organ for those questions of wider interest which did not involve territorial alterations. Thus the Committees that had been appointed to deal with the questions of international rivers, precedence of ambassadors, etc., reported to it; while it also received the report of the Conference on the Slave Trade, and drew up a formal declaration on the subject. The Swiss Committee also reported to the Committee of Eight, which approved the final declaration on the subject, though the Committee of Five also considered this question. The Committee of Eight was also chosen as the organ of the declaration of March 13 against Napoleon, when it spoke in the name of all Europe, much to the discontent of some of the minor Powers.[1] Its protocol of May 13 on this subject was also subsequently signed by many of the minor Powers. In short, the Committee of Eight was apparently intended to be used, when it was necessary, to consider subjects affecting the general interests of all Europe; and it was to this Committee that the Final Act, when the Committee of Five had prepared it, was given for signature.

Lastly, it must be remembered that, side by side with the Committee of Five, and in no way constituted by it or depending on it, sat the Committee to consider the German Constitution.[2] The original Committee, which held thirteen meetings, perished in the midst of the dissensions of November. It was not until May 23 that a new Conference was instituted, containing representatives of all the minor States of Germany except Württemberg, which would have nothing to do with it. In the time at its disposal it could not work out a full scheme. It merely created a central body and laid down some general principles; and the Constitution of Germany was not completed until the final meeting at Vienna five years afterwards. But it is noteworthy that both the Germanic Committees were separate from the rest of the organisation of the Congress. Their only connection with the central Committees was the incorporation of some of the articles they had agreed upon in the Final Act, which set the seal of the Great Powers on their work.

It is seen, therefore, that the Congress of Vienna as a Congress of all Europe was never constituted. It remained a Congress of the Great Powers, who for their convenience had

---

[1] Münster, *op. cit.*, p. 228; 'It is reasonably asked by what right the eight Powers signing the Treaty of Paris speak in the name of all the Sovereigns of Europe, whom they were not at the trouble of consulting; by what right Sweden and Portugal decide for Sardinia, Denmark, the Low Countries, or Bavaria. The Kings of Bavaria and Denmark, both present, have with reason regarded this omission as an insult.'

[2] See below, Section 28.

summoned the smaller Powers of Europe to meet them. idea of a constituent assembly, imagined by some, wlTalleyrand had tried to use for his own purposes, was found to be impossible. The large number of small States made such an assembly impracticable in any case. But the wishes of the masters of Europe were from the first clear and unbending on this point. They considered themselves as 'Europe', and at the Congress they asserted successfully the ascendency of the Great Powers. The smaller States were only to be admitted at such times and on such terms as suited those who had great resources and armies at their command.

Section 19. *The Preparation of the Form of the Treaty*

The exact form in which the treaty should be finally drawn up was a subject of controversy almost to the close of the Congress. The problem was not an easy one, and on the whole it was solved in a manner which did credit to the diplomatists concerned. In this question, as in so many others, it was the insistence of the British plenipotentiaries which finally settled the points in dispute. When the discussions in January and February had resulted in agreement on the territorial arrangements in Germany and Poland, the Committee of Five nominated a *Commission de rédaction*, which contained mostly the same members as the Statistical Commission, which had just been investigating the territories in dispute. This reported on February 10 a plan for the first thirty-two articles of a treaty, which covered the points already discussed; and this scheme was approved by the plenipotentiaries at this and the next Conference.[1] The actual drafting of the articles had, however, yet to be undertaken. Many of these had been agreed to and consigned to the protocols by the end of February, and the final *rédaction* could now be begun.

[1] D'Angeberg, 707, 737, 774, 776.

On March 6, therefore, the Committee of Five appointed two chief draftsmen (Gentz and La Besnardière) to draw up a treaty from the protocols; and a Committee, containing a representative of each of the five Great Powers, was associated with them in the work. It was decided, however, to refer the matter to the Committee of Eight; and in this Committee a third chief draftsman was added in the person of Anstett, a Russian, and a representative of each of the eight Powers was appointed to supervise the work. Anstett, however, was ill, and La Besnardière was unable to work, so moved was he by the return of Napoleon. To Gentz alone, therefore, was left the task of drawing up the form of the treaty, and he submitted a scheme at the end of March.[1]

The decision to have one general treaty had not, however, been arrived at without some controversy. The idea had been persistently opposed by the Russians, who wished merely to have each separate transaction recorded in its own treaty. But Castlereagh insisted on the inclusion of all the agreements in the general treaty; and this view was upheld with success by Wellington, who, however, never realised all the difficulties of securing the *rédaction* of so formidable an instrument, and expected everything to be concluded in a very short space of time.[2] Difficulties, however, continued to arise; and, now that Europe was again being organised for battle against Napoleon, it was impossible to delay the settlement of the final agreements on the territorial arrangements by formal treaty between the Powers specially interested.[3] Separate treaties were therefore concluded concerning Poland between Russia, Prussia, and

---

[1] Clancarty to Castlereagh, April 1, 1815, F.O. Continent 7. *B. and F.S.P.*, II; Gentz, *Dépêches Inédites*, p. 162. Stein also drew up a plan for the treaty. Pertz, G. H., *Das Leben des Ministers Freiherrn von Stein*, VI, 2, 13.

[2] On March 12 he thought the final treaty would be signed by the end of the month, and when he left he only gave it to the middle of April.

[3] This course was urged by Castlereagh as soon as he received news of Napoleon's escape. *W.S.D.*, IX, 590.

Austria, Great Britain acceding, but not being a principal party, since Castlereagh wanted to appear as little responsible as possible for the Polish partitions. A similar treaty was concluded as to Saxony, and this example was followed in other matters as they became ripe for a full settlement; while on other questions, such as the slave trade, a form of declaration was drawn up. The Russian plenipotentiaries used this situation to attempt once more to avoid the signing of a general treaty, but Clancarty insisted on concluding it before the diplomatists separated. He suspected, not without reason, that Russia wished to avoid committing herself at this moment on several questions which would necessarily be included in the Final Act. He carried the day, assisted by the Prussians, who wanted as much guarantee for their new possessions as possible, and by Talleyrand, who wanted Louis XVIII's name on a public treaty. By a protocol of May 26 Gentz was again entrusted with the *rédaction* of the general treaty, while Clancarty and Humboldt were appointed to watch in the interests of the other Powers.[1]

A treaty of 110 articles was thus drawn up. Not all the separate agreements were included in the articles, but the other treaties and declarations were added as appendices, and given the same force as if they had been embodied in the treaty itself. The actual subjects chosen for insertion in the general treaty were somewhat arbitrarily selected, but were intended to include all the most important territorial changes. At the last moment Metternich insisted on the basis of the German Confederation being included in the treaty, which necessitated the addition of eleven articles, the total being thus 121.

Next came the question as to who was to sign the instrument thus prepared. The mere labour of preparing copies would alone have prevented all the sovereign States affected being made

[1] Münster, *op. cit.*, 268; Clancarty to Wellington, May 26, 1815, *W.S.D.*, X, 380; Protocol of May 26, 1815, *B. and F.S.P.*, II, 738; Talleyrand to Louis XVIII, May 23 and 27, 1815. Pallain, pp. 426, 428; Talleyrand, *Mémoires*, III, 193; Gentz, *Dépêches Inédites*, p. 165.

parties.[1] Many of the Powers had now no plenipotentiaries left at Vienna, while some would have been certain to raise objections. It was therefore decided to confine the signatures to the eight Powers, which, since Spain would have nothing to do with a treaty which it considered had entirely neglected its interests, meant seven Powers only.[2] On June 9 the plenipotentiaries of these seven Powers met and initialled all the articles except those concerning the German Constitution, which were not yet ready. The Russian plenipotentiaries, however, declared that they could not sign the treaty until Alexander had seen it in its completed form. There were no sinister motives in this refusal, which simply marked the subordination in which Alexander kept his Ministers. The other plenipotentiaries, and especially Clancarty, were, however, so dismayed at this news that Nesselrode set out in haste to get permission to sign.[3] Clancarty's anxiety on June 19, when a final sitting was held to affix the formal signatures, may therefore well be excused. Amid the sarcasms and scarcely hidden jeers of the other plenipotentiaries he insisted on re-reading the whole treaty and kept them waiting till midnight before he would sign.

'On ne peut pas être trop scrupuleux,' he said, 'dans cette affaire; cet instrument sera un titre de famille pour ceux qui y ont mis leur nom.'[4]

---

[1] It took twenty-six secretaries, working from morning to night, to prepare a copy of the treaty. Klinkowström, p. 538

[2] Clancarty to Castlereagh, June 10, 1815, F.O. Continent 19; Münster, *op. cit.*, p. 274; 'It is agreed that the Powers subscribing the Treaty of Paris should alone sign, and that the rest of the Courts should accede separately. This distinction is arbitrary in itself, and even unsound. . . . But it was difficult to find another way of diminishing the number and the intricacy of the ratifications, which would amount to more than 1,600 if all the Courts had signed and exchanged formal Acts.'

[3] Clancarty to Castlereagh, *ibid.*; 'We strongly represented not only the inconvenience and delay which would be thus incurred but the incalculably pernicious consequences which must infallibly follow from the appearance thus afforded of difference and disunion, or at least of strong jealousies being prevalent among the Allies.'   [4] Klinkowström, p. 537.

As it was, permission for the Russians to sign did not arrive till eight days later, and the treaty was not finally completed till June 26. All the Great Powers, as well as Portugal and Sweden, had then signed, the last-named, however, protesting against certain articles, notably that which restored Ferdinand to Naples. A protest by Consalvi on behalf of the Papal Court, which dealt mainly with the neglect of the Pope's temporal interests, did nothing to lower the importance of the Final Act in public opinion.

A general instrument had thus been created which served as a basis for the international life of Europe for nearly fifty years. It was of first-class importance that the insistence of the British and French plenipotentiaries on this form of treaty had met with success. By uniting all the separate instruments in the *Acte final* a much more solemn document was constructed than would have been a collection of treaties and declarations, some of which would have lacked the signature of many of the Powers. By the procedure adopted, each Power, in order to obtain from the Vienna Treaty the protection and guarantee of its own special interests, had also to agree to the rest, however much it might object to any particular portion of it. As almost every State was affected by the treaty, the result was to place the Vienna settlement in a special position, which no other instrument has ever attained. The rest of Europe was invited to sign the treaty by accession. Several of the minor Powers refused for some time, either because they violently disagreed with some of the stipulations, or because there were still some arrangements outstanding which they desired to see completed before they committed themselves. But, in the end, practically the whole of Europe acceded to the treaty; and its stipulations were thus in a special way agreed to, and in a sense guaranteed by all the sovereign States of Europe. The Pope and the Sultan were, of course, exceptions, both for rather petty reasons, and both, ultimately, much to their own disadvantage.

As has been seen, when the Congress met there had been in Europe a desire to give the new arrangements something more than the form of a treaty—a desire to add such special guarantees of the whole as would intimidate any Power which might try to overthrow it. Such an attempt to give permanence to a territorial settlement which was defensible solely by the principle of the balance of power would, in any case, have been doomed to failure. But the idea formally brought forward by Castlereagh, and warmly welcomed by the Emperor of Russia, is worthy of more extended consideration as the first attempt by European statesmen to make their agreements permanent.

Section 20. *The Project of a Special Guarantee of the Vienna Treaty*

This project for a special guarantee of the Vienna Treaty was brought forward by Castlereagh just before his departure. After the crisis of the Polish-Saxon question was ended, both the contending parties wished to renew their alliances with Castlereagh before he left Vienna. The Tsar, who knew of the secret treaty of January 3, 1815, rather cleverly pressed for a renewal of the Quadruple Alliance, while Metternich and Talleyrand wished to conclude further secret engagements. Castlereagh, in order to check both these proposals, and at the same time give a special safeguard to that territorial equilibrium which he hoped had been successfully established, brought forward a scheme for a special declaration to safeguard the arrangements which had cost so much effort to conclude.

'I submitted to the Emperor,' he reported, 'that the best alliance that could be formed in the present state of Europe was that the Powers who had made the peace should, by a public declaration at the close of the Congress, announce to Europe, whatever difference may have existed in the details, their determination to uphold and support the arrangements agreed upon; and, further, their determination to unite their influence, and if necessary their arms, against the Power that should attempt to disturb it.'[1]

Alexander had himself long ago put forward ideas not altogether dissimilar,[2] and he professed himself enthusiastic over the proposal.

Gentz was accordingly asked to draw up the declaration, and produced a verbose and not very happily worded document.[3] It would, however, have bound the Powers to oppose, with arms if necessary, any attempt to overthrow 'l'ordre établi' by the treaty; and Castlereagh at this time undoubtedly expected the declaration to be issued to the world.[4]

Castlereagh united this scheme with a project for obtaining in the Vienna treaty a guarantee of the integrity of the Ottoman Empire. The Porte, genuinely alarmed at the increase of Russian power, had been pressing this idea on both the British and Austrian Governments for some time.[5] Metternich had been unwilling to risk a proposal of this nature in the state of his relations with Russia, but Castlereagh seized this opportunity to bring the matter before Alexander. If the Tsar's new possessions in Poland were to receive the special guarantee of Europe, a guarantee of those of the Porte might be claimed as a *quid pro quo*. Alexander could not very well refuse, without betraying designs which were in direct contradiction to the

---

[1] Castlereagh to Liverpool, Feb. 13, 1815, F.O. Continent 7.
[2] Alison Phillips, *op. cit.*, p. 32.
[3] D'Angeberg, p. 864; Klinkowström, p. 529.
[4] Castlereagh, Circular Despatch, Feb. 13, 1815; 'It affords me great satisfaction to acquaint you that there is every prospect of the Congress terminating with a general accord and guarantee between the Great Powers of Europe, with a determination to support the arrangements agreed upon, and to turn the general influence, and if necessary the general arms against the Power that shall first attempt to disturb the Continental peace.' F.O. Continent 8. See also the 'Déclaration des Plénipotentiaries de la Grande-Bretagne par rapport à la garantie', annexed to the protocol of February 11; D'Angeberg, p. 1860.
[5] Sir Robert Liston to Castlereagh, Mar. 10, July 25, 1815, F.O. Turkey 82; Gentz, *Dépêches Inédites*, I, 121, 142.

lofty principles he was joining in defending. But he made it a condition that the points in dispute between Russia and the Porte, which had arisen since the hastily-executed Treaty of Bucarest (1812), should first be settled through the intervention of Great Britain, France, and Austria; and he also wished that something should be done to prevent the massacre of the Serbs, to which the Turks had now turned their energies.[1] These conditions were sufficient to make his consent useless; and, though the British Ambassador did his best to get the Porte to agree, the proposal was rejected even before the news of Napoleon's return reached Constantinople.[2]

This rebuff was not likely to make England press the general scheme; and the return of Napoleon, which brought about a renewal of the Quadruple Alliance, inevitably increased the difficulties of guaranteeing the new order in Europe. It is, however, surprising to find Russia, at a later stage, pressing the adoption of a special guarantee, while Austria and England opposed it.[3] The motives which led to this result are not fully known, but they appear to have been based on the uncertainty of the situation in Europe and the failure of the negotiations concerning Turkey. The Final Act, therefore, had no greater sanction than any other treaty. The impression produced on Alexander by the transaction was, however, immense. It awoke ideas that had been in his mind at previous epochs,

[1] Castlereagh to Liston, Feb. 14, 1815, F.O. Continent 12; Fournier, *Die Geheimpolizei, etc.*, p. 411, where the report of the Turkish representative, Mavrojeni, is given; Wellington to Castlereagh, Feb. 25, 1815, *W.S.D.* IX, 578.

[2] Liston to Wellington, Mar. 25, Apr. 4, 1815, F.O. Continent Archives 26, F.O. Miscellaneous 95/23.

[3] See a paper on 'Some Aspects of Castlereagh's Foreign Policy' by the present writer in the Transactions of the Royal Historical Society, 3rd series, vol. VI, Nov. 16, 1911. A subsequent examination of the Petrograd Archives confirms the fact that Clancarty refused to agree to the scheme at a later date; Nesselrode to Lieven, June 5-17, 1815. The refusal was attributed by the Russians to secret projects between Austria and England on the model of the treaty of January 3, 1815.

and these, twisted into a strange shape by the emotional crisis he was to experience during the course of the year, produced the strange document of the Holy Alliance.[1] The Holy Alliance, however, was drawn up on lines very different from those of Castlereagh's scheme, which was simply a territorial guarantee. It should also be noted that, while Castlereagh's scheme was specially suited to protect the interests of the Porte, the Holy Alliance was so worded that only Christian sovereigns could sign it.

It may be well also to remember that, in the discussions that were to ensue during the period following the Congress of Vienna on the exact character of the treaties signed in his period, Castlereagh adopted the view that the Vienna Treaty was no more sacred and special than any other treaty which settled the limits of the European States. By that time he had learnt how difficult it was to guarantee territorial rights without at the same time touching upon internal questions. The extravagant schemes of Alexander had made him welcome the fact that the Treaty of Vienna was no European Alliance, but simply an ordinary treaty, the breach of which gave any Power affected the right to recourse to arms, but which implied no general promise on the part of Europe to come to its support.[2]

Section 21. The Method of Transacting Business. The Functions of the Committees. The Statistical Committee

The charge of idleness made against the Congress is, on the whole, unfounded. The real work could only be transacted by a comparatively small number of people, and these were most

---

[1] There can be no doubt that the idea of the Holy Alliance was given to Alexander by this proposal. Castlereagh was of that opinion (see Castlereagh to Liverpool, Sept. 28, 1815. *W.S.D.*, XI, 176), and the Tsar confessed as much to his religious confidant, Prince Golitzin, at a later date. Grand Duke Nicholas Michaelovitch, *L'Empereur Alexandre I er I.* 524.

[2] See Appendix VIII, p. 187. Memorandum presented to the Conference of Aix-la-Chapelle, Oct. 1818.

of the time overwhelmed with business. It was only the sovereigns, minor plenipotentiaries, and the mass of irresponsible visitors, who really had time to enjoy the daily routine of pleasure provided by the Austrian Court. The principal Ministers and their subordinates put in an appearance only when it was necessary for them to approach some royal personage or to meet some rival or ally. Metternich was the least industrious of the principal Ministers, as Gentz often complained, but the others never relaxed their efforts.

At the formal meetings of the Eight, held in Metternich's room, there were usually eighteen to twenty persons present; and the scene has been perpetuated in a picture by Isabey. Metternich was President of this Committee, and Gentz acted as its secretary; and in this sense they were President and Secretary of the Congress.[1] At the Committee of Five Wessenberg acted as protocolist. Gentz, however, and his subordinates kept what was substantially a 'Bureau de Protocole', which served as the business centre of the Congress; and Gentz expressly styled himself 'First Secretary of the Congress'.[2] The main business was, however, transacted informally. During the first four months the Ministers of the four Powers met nearly every morning at Metternich's for an informal conference. For some time also the three Sovereigns met in the afternoon to review the matters which had been discussed by their Ministers in the morning. It was necessary for innumerable private interviews to take place between the Ministers and the representatives of smaller Powers; and it was in these private conferences that the decisions on the big questions

[1] Metternich, however, disclaimed the title of 'President of the Congress'. D'Angeberg, 197.

[2] Klinkowström, p. 538. One of Talleyrand's original ideas was the formation of a *Bureau de Protocole* for the Congress, which he suggested should be in charge of La Besnardière, Cook, the British Under-Secretary, and Binder, an Austrian diplomatist. The nationality of the three officials is significant. Münster, Sept. 2. 1814. Hanover Archives.

were arrived at. Castlereagh, especially, who was acting as mediator, scarcely allowed a single document to be exchanged between the Powers on the Polish-Saxon question without either preparing the way for it by an interview or smoothing away difficulties by personal explanations. The technical work by which the ideas and compromises of the Ministers were put into shape was managed by a small group of men. Of these the chief were Humboldt, who was mainly responsible for the numerous Prussian papers; Clancarty, who was one of the most industrious and conscientious workers at the Congress; Dalberg, who added the practical touches to Talleyrand's outbursts; La Besnardière, who composed many of his ablest papers; Wessenberg, who made up for Metternich's lack of industry; and Gentz, who drew up nearly all the most important declarations, drafted the treaty, and found time to send long despatches to the Hospodar of Wallachia. Both Prussia and Austria had also a number of capable civil servants who rendered invaluable service.

Special Committees.—As has been seen, various Committees[1] were set up to deal with special questions. These were constituted on no set principle, being appointed from time to time as circumstances required. The members of them were not always plenipotentiaries, minor officials being allowed to take part. The Committee of Five, the real Congress, however, kept so much of the work in its own hands that the total number of these Committees is surprisingly small, when the large number of subjects covered is considered. The Committees were all nominated by the Committee of Eight or the Committee of Five (except the German Committee, which arose of itself, and the Swiss Committee), and to these two directing Committees the sub-Committees reported—to the Committee of Eight if the subject were of a general nature, and to

[1] For details of the constitution of the Committees see also the paper on International Congresses, No. 154, Part II, Section 10.

the Committee of Five if territorial questions were concerned. The Committees consisted for the most part of representatives of the five Great Powers, though in one or two the minor Powers were also represented. Not all of the five Powers were, however, represented on all the Committees, only those specially interested having members.

The most important Committee was that on Switzerland, consisting of representatives of the four Powers, a French one being added later. It was appointed apparently by the Ministers of the four Powers, and met first formally on November 14, 1814.[1] It conferred with the Swiss representatives, and eventually reported to the Committee of Eight, but its territorial arrangements were also considered by the Committee of Five, altered, and referred back by them.[2] A Committee on Tuscany, appointed by the Committee of Eight, contained representatives of Spain and France, as well as of Austria, Russia, and England. There were also small Committees appointed to consider the transfer of Genoa to Sardinia and the complicated question of the Duchy of Bouillon.

Three Committees were also appointed by the Committee of Eight to deal with the three general questions brought before the Congress. That on the slave trade, however, was not allowed to call itself a Committee, but only a Conference. Spain and Portugal had members on it, as well as England and France, while Sweden, Russia, and Austria were also represented. The important Committee on international rivers at first consisted only of the Great Powers interested, but subsequently representatives of the smaller riparian Powers were added to it. Each of the eight Powers was represented on the Committee appointed to examine the relative status of European Powers and their diplomatic agents. These three

[1] D'Angeberg, 430. The exact occasion on which it was appointed is obscure.
[2] D'Angeberg, 735, 930, 932.

Committees reported to the Committee of Eight, and their reports were adopted by it.

The functions and constitution of the drafting Committee has already been considered.[1] The Statistical Committee, of which details are given below, was the only other formed. The total, not counting the Committee of Eight, and that of the Five, was only ten, including the German Committee. The small size of the directing Committee and the wish of the principal plenipotentiaries to keep affairs in their own hands accounts for the small number necessary to deal with so many complicated questions. It may be doubted if the efficiency of the Congress would have been increased by any further devolution of business. The territorial questions were all closely related, and needed consideration as a whole, and, if separated, would have constantly needed reference back to the Committee of Five.

One of the conspicuous successes of the Congress was the Statistical Committee. As has been stated, this Committee was one of Castlereagh's ideas, and it is difficult to see how the Congress could have come to any definite conclusion without it. There had already been considerable recrimination as to the population of the territories under discussion. The problem of the reconstruction of Prussia was largely an arithmetical one. The Committee was ordered to make a complete enumeration of all the territories conquered from Napoleon and his Allies. Martens, the international lawyer, acted as its secretary, but the chief work was done by Hoffmann, a Prussian statistician of deserved reputation; and the result was to establish, in the main, the Prussian figures. The sources on which the Commission drew were, of course, largely non-official, since a systematic census had never been taken of many territories. Nevertheless, the only serious difficulties were found in the enumeration of the Duchy of Warsaw, where a

[1] See above, Section 19.

mean between two disputed figures was accepted. The Commission was not appointed till December 24; and on January 19 it was able to furnish the Committee of Five with a report, which gave statistics of population of all the territories with which they were concerned. It had been originally the intention, both of Castlereagh and Metternich, that something more than a mere evaluation of numbers should be made, and that the riches of the respective provinces and the quality of their inhabitants should be taken into consideration.[1] But this view was successfully opposed by Prussia; and the Committee was eventually strictly enjoined not to take into consideration anything but the actual numbers. Talleyrand, indeed, made some protest against a valuation which reckoned an inhabitant of Poland and one of the rich territories of Saxony and the Rhine as of equal worth. But it was impossible to put these ideas into practice, as they would have introduced standards of value which could not be weighed by the statisticians. The result was, of course, to the advantage of Prussia.

Section 22. Espionage. The Social Life of the Congress

At Vienna there was in existence the most completely organised secret police in Europe;[2] not even Napoleon, with the help of Fouché, possessed a machine of such efficiency. When it was known that the Congress was to meet at Vienna, immense preparations were made to strengthen the personnel of this secret service. Not only was there engaged a large number of new agents in every class of society, but also a

[1] Castlereagh to Liverpool, Dec. 24, 1814, F.O. Continent 9 (see Appendix VII); Pallain, p. 201; D'Angeberg, p. 561. See C. Dupuis, *Le Principe d'Equilibre et le Concert européen*, pp. 60 ff.; F. von Arneth, *Johann Freiherr von Wessenberg*, I, 233. Münster also tried to use this Commission for political purposes.
[2] The activities at the Congress of the secret police have recently been revealed by two historians who have had access to the documents of the Ministry of the Interior in Vienna. See Fournier (A.), *Die Geheimpolizei au dem Wiener Kongress;* Weil (M. H.), *Les Dessous du Congrès de Vienne*, 2 vols.

number of volunteers, many of the highest rank, were
in the service of the Emperor by Hager, the industrio
of the secret police. From the opening of the Congre
close the vigilance of these agents never relaxed. The waste-
paper baskets of the diplomatists, whose contents were
obtained by servants placed there for the purpose, provided a
rich store of material. Every letter that came through the post
was, of course, opened. This was the usual custom, and known
to all diplomatists. If they sent anything by post which they
did not wish to be read, cipher was always used.[1] But the
Austrian police obtained, through the venality of couriers and
servants, many letters and notes which were thought to have
been despatched quite safely. A daily report of these documents
was sent to the Emperor by the chief of the secret police,
together with a record of a large number of conversations
which had been shared in or overheard by his agents. Even the
Austrian Court and Ministers were not exempt from this
espionage, which attempted to include in its meshes every
person of the slightest importance at Vienna.

By such means the police did find out a very great deal.
Their reports were, perhaps, most useful in furnishing details
of the relations of one person to another and in gauging the
public opinion of the Congress. The principal Ministers used
their own couriers, and thus their despatches were generally
safe, while the actual facts as to the most important transactions
were only known to a very few people. Still, a great many
very secret things were ascertained in this way.[2] The French

---

[1] But some ciphers were known. The Prussians obtained a copy of the
British cipher during the Napoleonic wars, and this fact was not discovered
till 1817. The Prussians also had the Austrian and Swedish cipher. F.O.
Prussia, 108, 114.
[2] For example, the French Consul at Leghorn was engaged in a plot to kidnap
Napoleon. His report, written in sympathetic ink between the lines of an
ostensibly commercial report, was torn up by Dalberg and thrown into the
waste-paper basket. It was secured and pieced together by the secret agents.

Embassy, in particular, was indiscreet; and the inner motives of Talleyrand's campaign were fully known to the Austrians. The relations of Alexander and Metternich with the Princess Bagratian and the Duchess de Sagan were reported in the greatest detail. A record of the visits that each important Minister paid or received each day was carefully made. How far the Austrian Foreign Office was able to use this information to advantage is not known. It appears possible that the Foreign Minister himself was not shown all of it, the reports being made direct to the Emperor. But it must have played a part in the decisions of November and December, when the issue of events was so uncertain; and it was very useful to Metternich in the deep game of intrigue he played in the Italian questions.

The secrets of the British mission were better guarded than those of any other mission at Vienna. The despatches were, of course, sent by couriers of tried fidelity. The only intercepts were some sent to Constantinople by Austrian couriers, the contents of which were already known to Metternich. Special instructions had also been given at the outset that the contents of the waste-paper baskets were to be carefully burnt; and the Embassy staff was specially warned against the dangers of Vienna social life. Thus, though at one time some of the Embassy servants seem to have been in the pay of the secret police, nothing of the slightest importance was found out. In short, Castlereagh anticipated the other diplomatists in precautions the necessity for which they only found out by experience.

The social side of the Vienna Congress has impressed itself on history, but its importance has been exaggerated. As has been pointed out, the unending series of balls, dinners, reviews, and fêtes did not greatly hinder the work of those whose industry was important. More serious were the rivalries of various ladies, in which Metternich and Alexander were involved, and which certainly increased the friction between them; and a certain amount of indiscreet conversation was due to the presence of so many women. Almost all the crowned heads and diplomatists brought their wives and other female relations to Vienna. Gentz's remark to Wessenberg:

'Rien de plus choquant que des généraux et des Ministres qui traînent avec eux des femmes (épouses surtout) dans leurs campagnes ou dans leurs missions',

may be considered just, but on the whole the results were less pernicious than might have been expected.

Section 23. Attempts to Influence the Decisions of the Congress through Public Opinion and the Home Governments

The endeavours of the diplomatists at Vienna to influence the course of events at the Congress by applying pressure elsewhere, either through public opinion or, in the case of Great Britain and France, through the home Governments, though on the whole entirely unsuccessful, are worthy of some notice. Public opinion in Germany was greatly stirred by the Saxon question and the problem of the German Constitution. There was a great journalistic battle on these subjects, in which all the Courts were concerned; and Talleyrand was suspected on more than one occasion of stirring up strife for his own purposes. It cannot, however, be said that they affected the decisions of the statesmen in any material degree. The Polish-Saxon question was settled purely on grounds of expediency; and the populations of Germany were transferred from one monarch to another, with scarcely the slightest reference to their wishes. The public opinion of the Habsburg Kingdom was directed (in the interests of Metternich) by Pilat in the *Oesterreichische Beobachter*, while Gentz disseminated his chief's views throughout Europe in articles which have been described as masterpieces of force and point.

H

Public opinion in England was closely watched, and especially the debates in the House of Commons. 'Tant que nous aurons un Parlement en Angleterre, il y aura une tribune pour toute l'Europe,' said Sir Sidney Smith at the Congress; and his words were repeated by a more profound publicist, the Abbé du Pradt.[1] The idea of using British public opinion to influence Castlereagh occurred to more than one Power. Talleyrand's notes were written to a certain extent with this end in view, though he appears to have taken no steps to act directly on the British Government.[2] Other diplomatists, however, wrote to the British press, amongst them the Bavarian Minister, who sent a letter to the *Morning Chronicle*, the principal opponent of the Government, under the pseudonym 'Saxon'.[3] Metternich might have been satisfied that he could not better the position which Castlereagh had assumed; but he tried to put pressure on the Prince Regent in the question of subsidies, only to meet with a complete rebuff. His Ambassador, Merveldt, was also ordered to insert articles in the press. Merveldt, however, who was not in Metternich's confidence, spent much time in trying to remove a deeply-rooted feeling in political circles that Austria was both financially and militarily exhausted, but he received a severe reproof for discussing the affairs of the Congress with Liverpool and the Prince Regent.[4]

It was the Russians, however, despite their failure in the early part of the year, who made the most determined attempt to undermine Castlereagh. Lieven was instructed, in a series of

[1] Du Pradt, *Congrès de Vienne*, I, 51.
[2] The Comte de la Chastre, his representative at London, was however, ordered to discuss the Neapolitan questions with the Ministry, and to try to find out their real opinions. To La Chastre, Dec. 14, 1814, Archives des Affaires Étrangères, Paris.
[3] Pfeffel to Wrede, Jan. 19, 1815; Fournier, *Die Geheimpolizei, etc.*, p. 365.
[4] Merveldt to Metternich, Sept. 22, Oct. 4, Dec. 2, 1814, Vienna Archives. The *Courier* was the paper chosen by Merveldt, and some money appears to have changed hands, though the Ambassador reported that 'English journalists affect not to be bought'.

despatches of December 1814, that Castlereagh was deliberately attempting to keep the Continent in a state of unrest in order to establish British influence in the rest of the world. He was ordered to obtain access to the members of the Cabinet who did not agree with Castlereagh's policy, especially Bathurst, Sidmouth, and Vansittart. The principal leaders of the Opposition were also to be sounded, while every effort was to be made to influence public opinion in a direction favourable to Russia's interests. For this purpose the principal journalists were to be approached, and views suitable to their different party opinions were to be suggested to them. Special stress was to be laid on the commercial advantages of a good understanding with Russia; and it was to be suggested that the liberties of the English people were themselves threatened by the support which the Foreign Minister was giving to the most reactionary Continental Powers. The various stages of the plan were carefully indicated. First there was to be the attempt to win over the Cabinet; only if this failed was recourse to be had to the Opposition and the press.[1]

Subsequent experience showed the Russians that they could do little by these means. Lieven reported that the best way of winning a more favourable position was to flatter the Prince Regent and to try to overcome the marked hostility he displayed towards the Russian Court. Orders were accordingly given for orders and uniforms to be sent for the delectation of His Royal Highness.[2] Special instructions were also sent, however, to watch over the discussions on the Polish question in the British Parliament, in order that the Russian point of view might be brought before the British public. The total effect of all this was not great. It is true that Castlereagh's policy was not popular with his colleagues, but they were

[1] Projet d'Instruction pour le Comte de Lieven, Dec. 1814, Petrograd Archives. See Martens (F.), *Recueil des Traités, etc.*, XI, 211.
[2] Nesselrode to Lieven, June 5-17, 1815, Petrograd Archives.

unable to influence him. As for public opinion in England, it was never sufficiently instructed and organised to produce any effect except in the question of the slave trade.

Castlereagh adopted with more success a similar policy towards Talleyrand. When he was not satisfied with the latter's attitude on the main points in dispute, he endeavoured to work on the King and Blacas through Wellington, hinting that, unless they agreed, he might be compelled to recognise Murat, and was able to get instructions sent which placed the Polish question for the moment before the Saxon one.[1] The readiness of his home Government to come into line with Great Britain undoubtedly affected Talleyrand's policy, but it was also at bottom his own real desire; and the total effect of the pressure cannot be said to have been of great importance. Metternich also endeavoured to circumvent Talleyrand by opening direct negotiations with Paris on the Italian question, and in this scheme he had considerable success. But events made this transaction of less importance than at one time seemed probable.[2] The truth was that nearly all that was most powerful in Europe was concentrated at the Congress, and distances were too great and the means of communication too slow for much effect to be produced by action elsewhere.

[1] Castlereagh to Liverpool, Oct. 24, 1814, F.O. Continent 7; *Correspondence*, X, 182, 184; *W.S.D.*, IX, 417, 493, 494.
[2] See below, Section 27.

Part Three

THE WORK OF THE CONGRESS

*Section 24. The Polish-Saxon Problem. The Failure of
Castlereagh's First Plan*

The decisions of the Congress of Vienna, as has been stated
above,[1] depended almost entirely on the settlement of the
Polish-Saxon question. As has been seen, Metternich and
Castlereagh hoped to achieve their ends in Poland by sacrificing
Saxony. If Poland could be saved from falling, almost entirely
brought under Russian rule, or, instead of this, partitioned
anew among the three Powers, Metternich appeared willing to
agree to the lesser evil of the absorption of the whole of
Saxony by Prussia. The territories in the west of Germany,
which were at the disposal of the Congress, could then be used
to a large extent to build up Holland and Hanover, and there
would be a surplus left to facilitate arrangements between
Austria, Bavaria, and Baden. Nothing had, however, as yet
been agreed to in writing. The plan depended on an informal
understanding between Hardenberg and Metternich, which
Castlereagh had enthusiastically supported. Two great obstacles
still stood in the way. Metternich had to fear the hostility of
an Austrian party, led by Stadion and Schwarzenberg; while
Hardenberg could not count on the support of his King
against the Tsar. There were also other questions in dispute
between the two German Powers which threatened to break
up their alliance.

Of all these difficulties Castlereagh was fully aware, but he

[1] See above, Section 14.

was under the impression that, by himself directing the negotiations, he could overcome them and force Russia to give way before the united opposition of her three allies. The instructions which Castlereagh certainly drew up for himself for the Congress of Vienna have never been discovered. The principles on which he acted are, however, not in doubt. His main object, as he told his Cabinet in November, was the establishment of a 'just equilibrium' in Europe;[1] and his conception of a 'just equilibrium' meant strengthening the centre of Europe against the East and the West. For this purpose he wished, not only for a strong Prussia, but also for an alliance between Prussia and Austria. The extension of Russian dominion over the whole of Poland he regarded as a real menace to the security of Central Europe. He would naturally have been glad to obtain an independent Poland. But, though he constantly rendered lip-service to this idea, it was never really contemplated as a possible solution either by him or by any other statesman at the Congress.

The attack against Alexander was begun, not by Hardenberg and Metternich, whose countries were mainly concerned, but by the English Minister acting as mediator. The Tsar condescended to argue his own case, which he first stated in an interview with Castlereagh at the end of September. Castlereagh, after establishing the fact that neither Russia nor her Allies were prepared to create an independent Poland, set out once more all the arguments against the Russian plan. Alexander's wish to give the Poles a Constitution would, he maintained, ensure the disaffection of such Poles as were still left under Prussian and Austrian rule; and he insisted that Alexander was defying the opinion of all Europe, including his own Russian subjects. In reply, Alexander said his policy

---

[1] Castlereagh to Liverpool, Nov. 11, 1814, F.O. Continent 8. See an article by the present writer on *England and the Polish-Saxon Problem at the Congress of Vienna* in Transactions of the Royal Historical Society, 3rd series, vol. VII.

was directed, not by Russian interests or his own ambition, but with a view to the happiness of the Poles and from a sense of 'moral duty'; and he hinted that public opinion in Great Britain approved his scheme. The impression he produced on Castlereagh, however, was that he was prepared to give up the idea of a Polish Kingdom if he could be allowed to retain Polish territory; and in an interview with Nesselrode next day, Castlereagh made it clear that he was not prepared to allow the odium of vetoing a Polish Constitution to fall on Great Britain. His objection, he said, to Alexander's plans lay more in the extension of territory which Russia would obtain than in the system by which she proposed to administer it.[1]

In order to set the Austrian and Prussian Ministers on a line of attack which he could himself support, he drew up a memorandum for their guidance, which based the opposition to Alexander's designs on the fact that they were contrary to the treaties signed in 1813. A second interview with Alexander followed. His plea that he had a duty to the Poles was turned by Castlereagh against him. 'I asked His Imperial Majesty how he distinguished between his duty to the Poles on one side of his line and on the other.' He insisted that the matter must be argued on grounds of expediency, which were the real motives animating the Powers concerned. It would be an injustice to Alexander to suppose that the interests of the Poles did not play a considerable part in his decisions; and he ultimately showed his good faith by granting them the Constitution which he had promised. But it was useless for him to plead his motive when he was not prepared to press it to its logical conclusion and re-establish a free Poland. It was Russian interests that governed the major decision against independence; and, on this point, Castlereagh fastened. Beaten in logic, Alexander could only rely on the argument of force. On this point, too, Castlereagh had an answer:

[1] Castlereagh to Liverpool, Oct. 2, F.O. Continent 7.

'The Emperor insinuated that the question could only end in one way, as he was in possession. I observed that it was very true His Imperial Majesty was in possession, and he must know that no one was less disposed than myself hostilely to dispute that possession; but I was sure His Imperial Majesty would not be satisfied to rest his pretensions on a title of conquest in opposition to the general sentiments of Europe.'

He transmitted the same day to the Tsar the memorandum he had drawn up for the guidance of Metternich and Hardenberg, together with a letter worded with the utmost frankness, so that there might be no doubt as to his opinions.[1] Meanwhile Alexander, in interviews with Talleyrand and Metternich, had adopted an even more menacing tone.[2] He made no secret of the fact that he intended to keep almost all the Duchy of Warsaw, and he would make no concessions of any kind.

The reason why Castlereagh had had to enter the lists single-handed, instead of the three Courts making a united protest, lay in the fact that the Austro-Prussian Alliance was not yet completed. On his arrival at Vienna, Castlereagh found that both Metternich and Hardenberg were loth to commit themselves. Metternich, indeed, talked loudly of war; but, in spite of the negotiations of the summer, he would not make in writing that definite offer of Saxony to Prussia which alone could induce her to join him in opposing Alexander; while Hardenberg dared take no step that would risk a rupture with Russia, lest he should be left without an ally. In these circumstances it was impossible to get either Power to oppose Alexander's threats by a show of force. But Castlereagh endeavoured to get them to combine to refuse to recognise Poland as Russian territory. He personally tried to influence the King of Prussia, but found him unwilling to oppose

[1] Castlereagh to Alexander, Oct. 12, 1814, *W.S.D.*, 330. The memorandum is printed in D'Angeberg. 265; *W.S.D.*, IX, 332.
[2] Pallain, *Correspondence inédite du Prince Talleyrand et du Roi Louis XVIII*, p. 18.

Alexander, though he admitted that he disapproved of his plans.

Castlereagh had more success with Metternich and Hardenberg, between whom he contrived an interview. Hardenberg explained very frankly that he could not join in exposing Russia while assurances as regards Saxony were still lacking. He promised, however, that if Austria and Great Britain would guarantee Saxony to Prussia he would unite with them 'to oppose such resistance as prudence might justify to Russian encroachments.' Metternich was without a fixed plan, and appeared already to have abandoned hope, but the insistence of Castlereagh at last induced him to agree.[1] Hardenberg immediately tried to obtain these promises in writing by a letter of October 9, which formally asked for the assent of England and Austria to the incorporation of Saxony in Prussia, as well as the acquisition of Mainz. Castlereagh gave immediate consent. Metternich still hesitated. Hardenberg pressed for reply, and at last, on October 22, Metternich agreed to the proposal.[2] He made it conditional, however, on the success of the Polish negotiations, and he declared that Bavaria must have Mainz. This was not sufficient to satisfy Hardenberg; and it was only by again bringing the two Ministers to a conference at his hotel that Castlereagh at last got them to agree, Hardenberg waiving the point of Mainz for the moment. Castlereagh himself drew up a plan for joint action. Alexander was to be threatened with a refusal of all the Powers to recognise his Polish acquisitions.

The suggestion of an independent Poland on a large scale was to be made, but this was not seriously intended. A partition of the Duchy of Warsaw between the three Eastern Powers

---

[1] Castelreagh to Liverpool, Oct. 9, 1814, F.O. Continent 7.

[2] Hardenberg to Metternich, Oct. 9, 1814, D'Angeberg, 1934; Castlereagh to Hardenberg, Oct. 11, 1814, *Ibid.*, 274, *W.S.D.*, IX, 339; Hardenberg to Metternich, Oct. 21, 1814, F.O. Continent 7; Metternich to Hardenberg, Oct. 22, 1814, D'Angeberg, 1939.

was the real objective.[1] The two Emperors and the King of Prussia were about to visit Buda-Pesth, and here Alexander was to be told of the united demand of his allies. Castlereagh had great hopes of success, but he made a fatal mistake in allowing the plan to be disclosed when he was not himself on the scene. Alexander showed that his reliance on his personal supremacy over the Prussian King was well founded. He attacked Metternich and Hardenberg with bitter fury in the presence of their masters; and, though the Emperor of Austria was firm, Frederick William immediately gave way. The whole edifice that Castlereagh had built up thus collapsed at the outset.[2] When Metternich, on their return to Vienna, asked the Prussian Minister to co-operate against Alexander, an evasive answer was returned, deprecating steps that might lead to hostilities, and suggesting various lines of compromise which Castlereagh was to submit to Alexander in the name of the two Powers. Even this answer was considered too anti-Russian by Frederick William.[3] Castlereagh and Metternich refused to consider joint discussions under these conditions. The rôle of mediator which the former wished to play was only possible if he had the two German Powers united behind him, while the Austrian Cabinet was now growing restive on the question of Saxony, with the result that Metternich's tone stiffened considerably. Castlereagh accordingly withdrew from the negotiations, and Metternich also intimated to Prussia that their joint action against Russia was at an end.[4]

In narrating his failure to his Cabinet, Castlereagh could only reiterate his opinion that, had it not been for the King of

[1] Castlereagh to Liverpool, Oct. 24, 1814, F.O. Continent 7.
[2] Castlereagh to Liverpool, Nov. 11, 1814, F.O. Continent 8.
[3] Metternich to Hardenberg, Nov. 2, 1814, D'Angeberg, 379; Hardenberg to Castlereagh, Nov. 7, 1814, F.O. Continent 8; Delbrück, *Friedrich Wilhelm III und Hardenberg auf dem Wiener Kongress, Zeitschrift*, LXIII, 263.
[4] Castlereagh to Liverpool, Nov. 21, 1814; Metternich to Hardenberg Nov. 12, 1814, F.O. Continent 8.

Prussia, the plan would have succeeded. The two Central Powers would then have been able to settle their difficulties on friendly terms, and it would have been easy to confront Alexander with a united Germany. He admitted that he had been led to take a more active share in the negotiations than he had thought was possible, but he felt that a mediator was necessary to unite Europe against Russia. All this had now failed, and he gave it as his opinion that,

'unless the Emperor of Russia can be brought to a more moderate and sound course of public conduct, the peace which we have so dearly purchased will be of short duration'.[1]

The Emperor meanwhile had been forced by the Poles to reply to Castlereagh's written communication. The memorandum was drawn up by Czartoryski, as Alexander had now ceased to employ any of the Russians on these transactions; and Nesselrode had so completely fallen into disfavour that it was expected every day that he would be superseded. In these circumstances it is not surprising that no suggestion of compromise was made. Castlereagh found himself under the necessity of replying, though he refused to treat Alexander as personally responsible for the memorandum. He reiterated the argument that Alexander was breaking the treaties of 1813; and, though the Poles insisted on an answer to this attack, Alexander forwarded it with a cold note asking that in future only official channels should be used. Neither Castlereagh nor Alexander had much reason to be satisfied with this method of conducting business. The Tsar had doubtless thought that, by negotiations in person, he could bear down Castlereagh's opposition, but the result was only to expose their differences. It may be noted, however, that, while Alexander permitted himself to indulge in ungovernable displays of temper towards Metternich, Hardenberg, and Talleyrand, he

[1] Castlereagh to Liverpool, Nov. 11, 1814, F.O. Continent 8; Nov. 18, *W.S.D.*, IX, 451.

never treated the British Minister otherwise than with the greatest courtesy.[1]

Where Castlereagh had failed it was not likely that Hardenberg would succeed, though for the sake of appearances it was necessary for him to make some attempt. He proposed to Alexander considerable cessions of his Polish territory, which would have given to Prussia the fortress of Thorn and the line of the river Wartha, and to Austria Cracow and the line of the river Nida. It was added that no further objection would be made to the Emperor's plans for a Polish Kingdom. The answer, delayed by Alexander's illness, was delivered by Czartoryski and Stein. The only concession made on the Polish frontier was to offer to make Thorn and Cracow free towns. At the same time even this concession was linked up with a demand that Saxony should be given to Prussia, and that Mainz should be a fortress of the Confederation.[2] The Russo-Prussian Alliance was thus demonstrated. Metternich could not accept such a proposal. His offer of Saxony to Prussia had been conditional on active co-operation against Alexander. It was now, therefore, withdrawn, and a complete deadlock ensured. The Saxon question now opened, especially in the inflamed state of public opinion in Germany, was a problem which appeared to have no solution; and, as Prussia had now to seek compensation in Germany for her losses in Poland, all the minor States were threatened.

Thus the first phase of the negotiation closed with a heavy defeat for Castlereagh. The scheme was his, and he had failed owing to Alexander's control of the Prussian King. Hardenberg had, indeed, acted against his own wishes, and bitterly repented of his folly in not settling the Polish frontiers in 1813.

---

[1] Alexander to Castlereagh, Oct. 30, 1814, *W.S.D.*, IX, 386; Castlereagh to Alexander, Nov. 4, 1814, *Ibid.*, 410; Alexander to Castelreagh, Nov. 21, 1814, *Ibid.*, 441. The last reply was delayed by the Emperor's illness.

[2] Castlereagh to Liverpool, Dec. 5, 1814, F.O. Continent 8; D'Angeberg, 485, 493; Münster, p. 194.

But Prussia was now relying on Russia to get Saxony, which was transferred from Russian to Prussian occupation in a manner which asserted in the eyes of Europe Prussia's intention to keep the whole of it.[1] The two German Powers were hopelessly at variance; and the situation which Castlereagh had feared from the first had arisen. The failure to check Russia had made Prussia and Austria irreconcilable rivals in Germany. For the moment Castlereagh could do nothing but let events take their course. As soon as he abandoned the conduct of the negotiations they became more embittered every day. Even the decencies of diplomacy were no longer observed, and military preparations were hastily begun by all the Great Powers.

Section 25. The Deadlock over Saxony. The Secret Treaty of January 3, 1815, between Austria, Great Britain, and France

Castlereagh was not long to remain a spectator of this impossible situation. He was soon called back to construct an entirely new combination. Beaten on the question of Poland, he was yet able to preserve the peace of Europe and build up a barrier, as he thought, to Russian power. In this he acted entirely on his own responsibility in a situation which cannot have been covered by his instructions, and, to a certain extent, in defiance of the wishes of his Cabinet. He received no official instructions of any importance from London until December. Liverpool carried on a voluminous private correspondence with him, throwing out suggestions, and giving some account of Parliamentary and public opinion at home; but it took

---

[1] Russia had pressed this transfer, to which Castlereagh and Metternich had given only provisional assent, at a much earlier date, in order to embroil Prussia with Austria. Hardenberg refused; but, acting on orders from Russia, Repnin, the Russian commander, issued a proclamation, which produced at Vienna exactly the effect desired by Alexander. Münster, p. 105.

between ten and twelve days for a courier to get to Vienna, and situations changed so rapidly that it was not possible for the Cabinet to exert much control. Its opinion on these European problems was, however, clear. On the Polish question it was exceedingly lukewarm, and it wished to have as little to do with this as possible. Liverpool was much afraid lest Great Britain should appear to oppose Polish independence, and, in the middle of October, he thought it advisable to press this point on Castlereagh's notice.[1] The account of Castlereagh's activities increased the alarm in London; and, at the end of October, Vansittart attacked Castlereagh's display of initiative in a memorandum which Liverpool said had made a deep impression on the Cabinet.[2] These warnings were repeated during the middle of November, and the dangers of war, and the necessity of at least an interval of peace, were pointed out again and again.[3]

Public opinion in favour of the independence of Saxony was now growing in London, and this was also expressed in Liverpool's letters;[4] but his main preoccupation was to keep Great Britain out of war. Castlereagh's despatches, recounting the failure of his policy of mediator, and hinting at hostilities, produced a definite instruction from the Cabinet. On November 27 an official despatch was sent to him, which contained the sentence:

> 'It is unnecessary for me to point out to you the impossibility of His Royal Highness consenting to involve this country in hostilities at this time for any of the objects which have been hitherto under discussion at Vienna.'[5]

Three weeks after he received this instruction, Castlereagh

[1] Liverpool to Castlereagh, Oct. 14, 1814, *W.S.D.*, IX, 342.
[2] Liverpool to Castlereagh, Oct. 28, 1814, *W.S.D.*, IX, 383.
[3] Liverpool to Castlereagh, Nov. 2, 18, 25, 1814, *W.S.D.*, IX, 402. 438, 285.
[4] Liverpool to Castlereagh, Nov. 18, 1814, *W.S.D.*, IX, 408.
[5] Bathurst to Castlereagh, Nov. 27, 1814, F.O. Continent 6.

signed a treaty which made definite provision for war. He did indeed alter his policy on the question of Saxony, but that was the natural outcome of the failure of the first plan. The offer of Saxony was conditional on the co-operation of Prussia in the question of Poland; and, when that was refused, the offer was withdrawn. The change arose, not from any instructions from home, but as a natural result of Castlereagh's attitude; he could not now desert Austria, whom he had compelled to follow the policy of co-operation with Prussia. It was indeed believed by many at the Congress that Castlereagh's change of policy was due to definite instructions from his Cabinet, whose timid attitude was fully known.[1] But, though this weakened Castlereagh's position, it did not affect his policy nor move him from the course he felt it necessary to follow.[2]

Castlereagh now regarded the Polish battle as lost. But, as relations between the three Eastern Powers grew more and more strained, it became evident that no settlement could be produced between them, except by the active interference of Great Britain. At the beginning of December, therefore, he began to attempt to reconcile the differences between Austria and Prussia. He joined, it is true, the Austrian side, but he never abandoned his policy of constructing a strong Prussia; and, as will be seen, he found it necessary to check her opponents after he had thwarted her in her main ambition. His first step, however, was to join Metternich in withdrawing his offer as to Saxony. In an interview with Hardenberg, he made it clear that he considered Austria could not be expected to give way on her Bohemian frontier now that she had lost her line of defence in Poland. She could not submit to see both Dresden and Cracow in the hands of Great Powers. The Prussian Chancellor, who now saw himself faced with the prospect of

---

[1] Münster, p. 201. The question is discussed in Delbrück, *op. cit.*, p. 249, and in Transactions of the Royal Historical Society, 3rd series, vol. VII, p. 61.
[2] Castlereagh to Liverpool, Dec 7, 1814, F.O. Continent 9.

being beaten both in Poland and Saxony, flared up and talked of war, but Castlereagh used his favourite argument that war was no remedy. How could Prussia expect to govern Saxony, he said, unless she had the consent of Europe? This language produced some effect, and Hardenberg promised to listen to an Austrian proposal. Castlereagh did his best to persuade Metternich to make this as conciliatory as possible. This Metternich promised to do, and both he and the Emperor of Austria had interviews with the Emperor of Russia to get him to make some concessions to facilitate the general arrangement.

In these circumstances there was some chance of a compromise; but, though Hardenberg and Metternich had been calmed down they were both surrounded by soldiers and officials who were exasperated by what they considerd the weakness of their chiefs.[1] 'I witness every day,' wrote Castlereagh, 'the astonishing tenacity with which all the Powers cling to the smallest point of separate interest',[2] and he was not sanguine. In a private letter to Liverpool, written at the same time, he recapitulated the chances of war, and discussed how far an armed mediation could prevent it. These fears proved only too well founded. The Austrian proposals, besides rejecting the offers of Thorn and Cracow as free towns, refused to allow Prussia to incorporate Saxony, and reserved the point of Mainz.[3] Hardenberg was so exasperated that he communicated to Alexander the whole of Metternich's confidential letters. Metternich in his turn had to defend himself and the result was a tremendous explosion and numerous hot and excited interviews between the Emperors and their

---

[1] Even Hudelist was now inveighing against Metternich's weakness; and Gentz had already drawn up a project for a Triple Alliance of Austria, Great Britain, and France. Münster to the Prince Regent, Nov. 27, 1814; Hanover Archives.

[2] Castlereagh to Liverpool, Dec. 7, 1814, F.O. Continent 8; Dec. 5, 1814, *W.S.D.*, IX, 463.

[3] Metternich to Hardenberg, Dec. 10, 1814, D'Angeberg, 505.

Ministers. But as Castlereagh phrased it, 'the climate of Russia is often the more serene after a good squall'; and Alexander, after vainly trying to get Metternich dismissed, made a personal cession to the Emperor of Austria by offering to give back the Tarnopol Circle of Galicia, which he had obtained at the Peace of 1809.[1]

But the two German Powers were still hopelessly divided. Hardenberg and Metternich, embittered by their mutual treachery, disputed every fact and figure, and compromise seemed hopeless. It was Talleyrand's opportunity. Had his hands been free he might now have made a great bargain, but he was already committed. The attitude he had adopted from the first at Vienna had made it necessary for him to join Castlereagh and Metternich. The steps which led to this situation go back to the interview of September, which laid the foundations of the Franco-British Alliance.

As has been seen, Castlereagh from the first adopted an attitude different from that of any of the other Ministers towards the rights of France in the Congress. Talleyrand's insistence on the point of Saxony, and his refusal to subordinate it to the question of Poland, had caused some friction between them.[2] But Castlereagh succeeded in limiting Talleyrand's public activities, and prevented him from bringing forward the Saxon question by inopportune notes. When he suspected that the French Minister was endeavouring to make some arrangement with the Tsar concerning Saxony, he took steps to act on the French Government through Wellington.[3] In this he had some success; and Talleyrand kept very quiet through all the critical stage of the negotiations, though he encouraged the popular movement in favour of Saxony in every quarter. When the Polish negotiations had broken

[1] Castlereagh to Liverpool, Dec. 17, 1814, *W.S.D.*, IX, 483.
[2] Castlereagh to Liverpool, Oct. 20. Oct. 24, 1814, F.O. Continent 7.
[3] See above, Section 23.

I

down, there was no longer any need to hold back. Castle-reagh, therefore, gradually grew more and more intimate in his relations with Talleyrand, without, however, giving him his whole confidence.[1] When the moment of crisis arrived, and the deadlock had to be solved by a show of force, he had France at his back, and he knew that his policy was one favoured by both the French and British Cabinets.

At the same time Metternich began to look to Talleyrand. Their relations had not been close until the month of December. But, after the storm between Hardenberg and Metternich, the latter sought Talleyrand's assistance. He appears to have been eager to anticipate Castlereagh, and on December 16 he made formal overtures to Talleyrand for joint action. Talleyrand's answer was a lofty defence of the integrity of Saxony, but in his private interviews he showed himself very accommodating. It was sufficient for him that the Alliance had broken to pieces, and he only required assurances on the question of Naples.[2] These could not be given him at once, but both Castlereagh and Metternich began to examine their archives to ascertain whether they could escape from the engagements made to Murat, while the French Government was asked to give proofs, if possible, of his treachery.[3]

Before, however, France was openly brought into the dis-

[1] Castlereagh to Wellington, Nov. 21, 1814, *W.S.D.*, IX, 447; 'I have not deemed it prudent to disclose to him my operations in detail, finding that he was not always discreet, and that I should lose influence in other quarters if I was understood to be in close confidence with the French Minister. I have endeavoured, however, to treat him with all proper regard, and to keep him generally informed of our endeavours to promote common objects. He is becoming infinitely more accommodating in our general conferences than at the outset.'

[2] Pallain, pp. 181, 183. Castlereagh to Liverpool, Dec. 18, 1814, F.O Continent 9, *W.S.D.*, IX, 483; Metternich to Talleyrand, Dec. 16, 1814, D'Angeberg, 1961; Talleyrand to Metternich, Dec. 19, 1813, D'Angeberg, 540.

[3] Castlereagh to Liverpool, Dec. 18, 1814, *W.S.D.*, IX, 485. For the develop-ment of the Neapolitan question see below, Section 27.

cussion, one more effort was made to come to a settlement through the intervention of Great Britain alone. This was directly requested by both Austria and Prussia, while Czartoryski, in the name of the Emperor of Russia, also pressed Castlereagh to accept the office of mediator. The result was that conferences were held between Castlereagh, Stein, Hardenberg, Humboldt, and Czartoryski in which a new proposal was broached. This plan, which had already been submitted to Metternich, was to compensate the King of Saxony with territory on the left bank of the Rhine, including Luxemburg, Trêves, and Bonn.

On December 21, in a long discussion, the Prussians in vain endeavoured to make Castlereagh yield on this point. Apart altogether from his engagements to Austria, Castlereagh did not want the left bank of the Rhine to be in the hands of a small Power, which he thought must come under the influence of France. He told the Prussians candidly that they must be content to acquire only a part of Saxony, and accept compensation elsewhere. At the same time he made it clear that he wished to make Prussia a powerful State, and, in order to win Russia over, he definitely promised that he would not press the Polish question further if Austria and Prussia consented to abandon their claims.[1] He had indeed hopes of some compromise, and finding that the dispute as to the statistics of populations caused much friction, he proposed the special Statistical Committee.[2] The appointment of this Committee revealed the attitude of Austria and England towards Talleyrand. The French Minister made it a point of honour that a French member should be appointed on it; and, though rather unwilling to expose his hand, Castlereagh acquiesced, and insisted that the concession should be made. He was anxious, however, not to allow a premature revelation of the close relations of himself and

[1] Castlereagh to Liverpool, Dec. 24, 1814, F.O. Continent 9.
[2] See above, Section 21.

Metternich with Talleyrand, which might give an excuse for an immediate rupture of relations on the part of Russia and Prussia. If the rupture was to come, he wished the other two Powers to furnish the excuse.[1]

Meanwhile, the Tsar was showing every sign of desiring a compromise. He interviewed the Emperor of Austria, and expressed his wish to finish everything amicably and without delay. The minor German Powers were now all rallying round Austria; and Metternich was coquetting with the idea of establishing a German Confederation under the Habsburgs without Prussia. Alexander brought matters to a head by desiring formal conferences on the Polish question. Castlereagh consented to attend[2] on condition that he was not supposed to be waiving his objection to the principle of partition, though agreeing to its expediency. The Conference which met on December 29, however, proceeded to discuss Saxony as well as Poland, and the time had come for Austria and England to reveal their connection with France. They demanded Talleyrand's admission to the formal conference. Prussia vehemently objected. The arguments used were formal; but all knew that the introduction of Talleyrand meant the end of Prussian hopes of obtaining all Saxony. The Prussians knew, too, that Alexander was weakening; and they attempted to force a settlement in their favour before it was too late. Hardenberg intimated that Prussia could not afford to remain longer in a state of provisional occupation of Saxony, and that, if recognition of her rights was refused, she would consider it as tantamount to a declaration of war. This truculent language produced an immense effect on Castlereagh.

'I took occasion to protest,' he reported, 'in the strongest terms against this principle as a most alarming and unheard-of menace:

[1] Castlereagh to Liverpool, Dec. 5, 1814, *W.S.D.*, IX, 511; Pallain, p. 199.
[2] Castlereagh to Liverpool, Dec. 25, 1814; F.O. Continent 9; Münster, p. 219.

that it should be competent for one Power to invade another, and by force compel a recognition which was founded upon no treaty, and where no attempt had been made to disturb the possession of the invading Power in the territory to which he laid claim. Such an insinuation might operate upon a Power trembling for its existence, but must have the contrary effect upon all that were alive to their own dignity; and I added that, if such a temper really prevailed, we were not deliberating in a state of independence, and it were better to break up the Congress.'[1]

Hardenberg's words were explained away, but the effect remained, and was increased by the knowledge that the Prussians were organising their army for the field and fortifying Dresden. Castlereagh's scruples about signing a treaty were overcome. He summoned Talleyrand and Metternich, and submitted a draft of a secret treaty which he had drawn up with his own hand. It was defensive in character, but made definite provision for war in case of attack by Prussia, on the model of the Chaumont Treaty against France. Any danger of its being used to extend French influence was guarded against by a clause stipulating that the Treaty of Paris was to regulate the future frontiers of Europe; and Holland's acquisition of the Low Countries was specially protected. Talleyrand and Metternich accepted this draft as it stood, though Castlereagh made it clear that he did not mean the treaty to prevent considerable concessions being made to Prussia in Saxony; and it was signed by all three on January 3. When it is remembered that Castlereagh's last official instruction had definitely forbidden him to involve his country in war, the boldness of this action will be realised. The news of the signing of the peace with America, which arrived on January 1, doubtless helped him to a decision, and he knew that his Cabinet would welcome an

---

[1] Castlereagh to Liverpool (Nos. 43, 44, 45), Jan.1, 1815, F.O. Continent 10. Pallain, p. 210. The draft of the treaty enclosed agrees almost entirely with the French text subsequently signed. Talleyrand made the translation.

alliance with France.[1] But the treaty meant war if Prussia did not give way; and in signing it on his own responsibility, Castlereagh showed how great was his courage and decision of character in moments of great emergency. In his private letter to Liverpool, he defended his action on the ground that, if war took place, Great Britain was bound to be involved, and it was necessary, therefore, to safeguard her interests.[2] Bavaria, Hanover, and Holland were all ready to sign; and there can be no doubt that, if war had broken out; all Europe would have joined in opposing Prussia, the behaviour of her soldiers having made her detested in every quarter. But the treaty was meant to prevent war, not to make it, and it succeeded in its object. In a few days all danger of a rupture was over.

Section 26. The Final Settlement of the German and Polish Territorial Questions

The effect of the treaty of January 3 was immediately apparent in the firm tone held by Metternich and Castlereagh in the second and third meetings of the four Powers. They declared peremptorily that they would not negotiate about Saxony until France had been admitted to the conferences. Hardenberg was at once intimidated, and went privately to Castlereagh to inform him that he would yield. He obtained in return an assurance that the settlement would be a real compromise, and would in no way depend on the consent of the King of Saxony himself; and Castlereagh secured Talleyrand's consent to this promise. More alarming was a revival of the proposal

[1] A memorandum had been drawn up by Bathurst urging an alliance with France (*W.S.D.*, IX, 480). There is no evidence that Castlereagh knew of this.

[2] Castlereagh to Liverpool, Jan. 2, 1815, *W.S.D.*, IX, 523. He seems to have had no doubt as to its reception; and his ascendancy over the Prime Minister was shown by the fact that Liverpool did not even call a full Cabinet to consider it, but ordered the ratification to be despatched post haste. Liverpool to Bathurst, Jan. 15, 1815, *W.S.D.*, IX. 535; Liverpool to Castlereagh, Jan. 15, 1815, *W.S.D.*, IX, 536.

to get the Saxon Monarch to consent to be transferred to a new kingdom, composed of the Rhine provinces. Castlereagh again declared this to be an impossible idea, and again got Talleyrand's support, sorely tempted though the latter perhaps was to establish a weak and subservient Power on the left bank of the Rhine.[1] Next day Castlereagh had an interview with Alexander in order to put an end, once for all, to this scheme, which some of the Prussians were pressing hard. He found the Emperor in a very peaceful mood. Rumours of the secret treaty had already reached him, and he challenged Castlereagh point-blank on the subject. The reply he received could have left him little doubt as to what had happened; and henceforward the Russian plenipotentiaries worked their hardest for a settlement.[2] In these circumstances the settlement of the Polish question advanced quickly; and the question of admitting France to the rest of the negotiations was also now only a matter of procedure. On January 9, Castlereagh secured it by a memorandum in which France was declared to be bound, through the second secret article of the Treaty of Paris, by the stipulations of the treaties of 1813: while it was definitely laid down that the King of Saxony's consent should not be considered necessary to any arrangements made. This memorandum was accepted by the others; Talleyrand gave a written consent; and the Committee of Five was thus constituted, and held its first meeting on January 12.[3]

[1] Castlereagh to Liverpool, Jan. 3, 1815, F.O. Continent 10; Jan. 5, 1815, *W.S.D.*, IX, 527.

[2] Castlereagh to Liverpool, Jan. 8, 1815, F.O. Continent 10. When, therefore, Napoleon sent to Alexander this treaty, which he found in the Paris archives on his return from Elba, it can have produced no surprise. Münster reported that Castlereagh's answer had dissipated the suspicion, and that rumours of the Alliance had died down (Münster to the Prince Regent, Jan. 22, 1815, Hanover Archives); but, in spite of Castlereagh's later fears, there can be no doubt that Alexander knew that a treaty had been made.

[3] *B. and F.S.P.*, II, 601; Talleyrand to Castlereagh, Jan. 8, 1815. F.O. Continent 10.

All immediate danger of war might now be considered as past, but the situation was still full of difficulty. It was not easy to find a sufficient number of inhabitants to compensate Prussia for the loss of a great portion of her Polish territories, if only a small part of Saxony was to be used for this purpose. The Austrian war party, feeling protected by the secret treaty, wished to press their victory home, and began to make inordinate demands. But Castlereagh had anticipated this situation. Having prevented Prussia from dictating terms to Europe, he had no intention of allowing the Austrians to make demands which would have been unattainable without his assistance. In the final stage of the negotiations, therefore, Castlereagh was engaged more in combating the extravagant pretensions of all sides than in merely supporting his own special allies. The construction of a powerful Prussia was, in his eyes, one of the essentials of the equilibrium of Europe; and it was largely by his assistance that she obtained so great an extension of territory. In the task of producing a territorial settlement he had now to work with feverish haste. Liverpool was pressing him by every courier to come back and defend the Tory Minister in the House of Commons. But he had no intention of leaving Vienna until the main problems were settled. For six weeks he worked with immense energy, keeping the conduct of the negotiations almost entirely in his own hands, acting as a real mediator, and by persuasion and firmness obtaining concessions from all sides, until at last an agreement had been produced on all the main questions.

The Austrian soldiers wished to deprive Prussia of Torgau on the Elbe as well as Erfurt, and Metternich was forced to second their demands. To these pretensions, urged by Stadion and Schwarzenberg, Castlereagh opposed an uncompromising negative. Austria's strength against a united Prussia and Russia must lie he said, in the support of her allies; against Prussia alone she was strong enough to stand, and he could not admit that

Saxony was to be considered as a State in the Austrian orbit. He told Metternich frankly that he would not support him in these strategical details, and, when he found that the Austrian Minister could not control his subordinates, he went to the Emperor himself. He found the latter fully determined to support the militarists, while Talleyrand joined Metternich in the endeavour to keep as much as possible of Saxony out of Prussian hands. Castlereagh, however, refused to 'sacrifice the peace of Europe for two or three hundred thousand subjects more or less'; and, after a long wrangle, he at last made Metternich give way, and secured a proposal which he thought he could support.[1]

It was now necessary to get Prussian consent to this offer. Hardenberg asserted that he dared not return to Berlin without Leipzig. Castlereagh retorted that the feelings of Berlin were not so material as the public opinion of the rest of Europe, and that a partition which separated Leipzig from Dresden was just what sound policy ought to avoid. Hardenberg remained unconvinced; and it was obvious that the pressure of the Prussian militarists was being exercised on him in the same way as Metternich was being coerced by the Austrian soldiers. Castlereagh, therefore, approached the King of Prussia himself. In an interview, which he described as 'the most painful in all respects that it has been my fate to undergo since I have been upon the Continent', he endeavoured to win his consent to the loss of Leipzig. This stormy interview produced no result; and a new deadlock threatened once more the peace of Europe. In this extremity Castlereagh turned to Russia. Alexander was exceedingly anxious for a compromise; but, when he was pressed for further concessions to assist the general

[1] Castlereagh to Liverpool, Jan. 11, 22, 29, 1815, F.O. Continent 10 and 11; Metternich to Schwarzenberg, Jan. 27, 1815; Klinkowström, p. 823; Münster, p. 222; D'Angeberg, p. 677; Fournier, *Die Geheimpolizei, etc.,* p. 349.

arrangement, he again pleaded his duty to the Poles. The reply was that Polish discontent could be easily overcome by uniting more of Russian Poland to the new kingdom. These arguments at last extracted Alexander's consent to the cession of the fortress of Thorn and a *rayon* round it to Prussia. With this bribe Castlereagh succeeded in obtaining the Prussians' consent to the loss of Leipzig, and the main difficulty was overcome. Prussia was, however, still intent on retaining more of Saxony than Austria would allow. In these circumstances Castlereagh, on his own responsibility, made Hanover and Holland reduce their claims to territory, so that Prussia might receive further compensation to the west of Germany; and by this bold exercise of authority he at last succeeded in producing an arrangement which all the Great Powers could accept.[1] By February 6, therefore, he was able to announce 'the territorial arrangements on this side of the Alps as, in fact, settled in all their essential features'. It cannot be doubted that this result was very largely due to the energy, firmness, and diplomatic skill of the British Minister.

After Castlereagh's departure there was no subject of controversy likely to disturb the peace of Europe; and, though the return of Napoleon brought new subjects for deliberation, yet it also furnished another reason for hastening the close. Yet the Congress lasted four months longer. The final arrangements as to Germany were hindered by a long struggle between Austria and Bavaria as to the town of Salzburg; and this matter was not finally solved until long after the signature of the Vienna Treaty. Both the settlement of Italy and the construction of the German Confederation progressed slowly. In this last phase Metternich took the lead in all matters not specially concerned with the prosecution of the war. But his energy was not equal to the demands on it; and, when he was dilatory, others had perforce to mark time. To a certain extent he deliberately

[1] Castlereagh to Liverpool, Feb. 6, 1815, F.O. Continent 11; Gagern, II, 124.

delayed matters in order to give time for new combinations to appear more suited to his designs.

All this bargaining produced a settlement in Central Europe which almost entirely subordinated considerations of nationality to the idea of the balance of power and strategical necessities; yet, if this was so, a great advance on previous conditions had been made, even in respect to national interests in the case of Poland. Though Posnania and the outlet to the sea at Dantzig remained in Prussian hands and Galicia was retained by Austria, Cracow remaining a free city, the mass of Polish territory remained intact under Russian sovereignty; and, though the idea of associating with the Duchy of Warsaw any portion of the old Polish territories now incorporated in the Russian Empire was abandoned, the rest was made into a kingdom which was soon to be endowed with a Constitution. Further, all the Powers had found themselves forced to recognise in theory the principle of Polish independence, though they had never the slightest intention of sacrificing their national interests to it. Castlereagh also, before he left, addressed a circular to all the Ministers, solemnly affirming his preference for a free Poland, and admonishing the three Eastern Powers that, only if the Poles were treated as Poles, was their future happiness and loyalty likely to be of long duration.[1] Both Prussia and Austria, as well as Russia, were forced to subscribe to these sentiments; and the final treaties in theory secured to all the Poles a separate administration. It must be admitted, however, that Castlereagh's declaration was made mainly with the view of being produced in the British Parliament; and, except Alexander and one or two of his advisers, none of

---

[1] Castlereagh to Liverpool, Jan. 11, 1815, F.O. Continent 10; 'I am convinced that the only hope of tranquillity now in Poland, and especially of preserving to Austria and Prussia their portions of that kingdom, is for the two latter States to adopt a Polish system of administration as a defence against the inroads of the Russian policy.' The note and replies are in *B. and F.S.P.*, II, 642.

the statesmen at the Congress were prepared to risk anything substantial for the sake of conciliating Polish national sentiment.

In Germany, Prussia obtained about two-fifths of Saxony, containing about 850,000 subjects, and including the Elbe fortresses, while she also obtained the main share of the left bank of the Rhine and the Duchy of Westphalia. The new Kingdom of the Netherlands had to be content with a small extension of territory beyond the Meuse. Castlereagh had, in fact, sacrificed the project of making a large Holland to the necessity of finding compensation for Prussia; and the attitude of Münster contributed to this result. The ancient Belgian province of Luxemburg was actually severed from the new realm. Prussia wished for the possessions of King William, i.e. the Nassau principalities of Dillenburg, Siegen and Dietz; and the greater part of Luxemburg (a part was retained by Prussia) was given to the King, in exchange for his German principalities, he receiving the title of Grand-Duke, and the Grand-Duchy becoming a sovereign State of the German Confederation. The town of Luxemburg itself was regarded as a federal fortress, and received a Prussian garrison.

The idea of creating a great Hanover was also abandoned, though she was raised to the dignity of a kingdom. Her acquisition of East Frisia was, however, considered important and bitterly lamented by some of the Prussians, while she obtained other valuable accessions of territory.[1] But the British Ministers

[1] Castlereagh to Liverpool, Feb. 13, 1915, F.O. Continent 12; 'The Hanoverian arrangement will not only give that Power the command of the Ems, but place it in direct contact with Holland throughout the greater part of its eastern frontier—an arrangement which, in a European point of view, must be considered of the utmost importance for the purpose of strengthening Holland and of securing the Low Countries. The general arrangement of the Prince of Orange's interests has given great satisfaction to his Ministers here; and I trust by his contiguity with Hanover, with Prussia advanced beyond the Rhine, and with Bavaria on the other flank, a better defence has been provided for Germany than has existed at a former period of her history.'

were anxious that the old charge of sacrificing British interests for the continental possessions of the royal house should not be revived; and Castlereagh had no scruples in cutting down her increase of territory when it was needed to compensate Prussia. Between the two, Prussia got a solid block of territory in the west, though she failed to secure a line of territory uniting it to Brandenburg as had been planned. Swedish Pomerania, the last relics of an old domination, also fell to her; Denmark, to whom it had been promised, being forced to accept in its stead Lauenburg, which Hanover had made great efforts to regain, and a monetary indemnity, which was partly a compensation for Heligoland.

Prussia's gains were thus of far more importance than the Polish territory she had lost; and one of the chief results of the Congress of Vienna was to establish her preponderance in the north of Germany. This reconstruction must be largely attributed to Castlereagh, for without his insistence Austria and France would never have consented to give her so much, what ever had been the fate of the Polish provinces.

Austria, meanwhile, though she regained Tirol and Salzburg from Bavaria, had retired from Germany to a large extent, and abandoned all share in the defence of the west. Stadion lamented that she had ceased to be a German power. She still, however, maintained her ascendency in the German Confederation, while her territorial power was increased in Italy. Bavaria, though she was not allowed to hold Mainz, which was made a fortress of the Confederation, was given the Lower Palatinate, which brought her into contact with Alsace. The series of exchanges between her and Baden and Austria were not, however, fully concluded until three years later. This individual bargaining was, indeed, never fully completed, and produced some strange compromises on the map of Germany. Such points as were left by the Congress to be settled by the Powers concerned were, in fact, more unsatisfactorily handled than any others.

Section 27. The Italian Problem. Murat, Spain, and Portugal

The Italian States were the subject of an intricate and sustained diplomatic duel between Talleyrand and Metternich, in which the former suffered heavy defeat.[1] While this was largely due to circumstances over which he had no control, the situation was one in which Metternich's subtle dishonesty found an ideal opportunity; and he used it to great advantage. Austria had already secured for herself both Venetia and Lombardy by the Treaty of Paris.[2] But Metternich intended, if possible, to make her influence dominant in the whole Peninsula, and to perpetuate the victory of Habsburg over Bourbon.

The problem revolved round Murat, King Joachim Napoleon of Naples, whose throne had been guaranteed by Austria in unequivocal language in a treaty of January 11, 1814. Great advantages had been obtained by this treaty; for Murat's desertion of Napoleon resulted in the collapse of the resistance made by Eugène Beauharnais in the north. Both Great Britain and Russia had assented to Austria's action; and the former had immediately abandoned the attack on the mainland which she was organising from her base in Sicily; but they did not enter into diplomatic relations with Murat or sign treaties with him. As to the rest of Italy, it had been agreed at Paris that Genoa should be incorporated in Piedmont, while the Duchies of Parma, Piacenza and Guastalla were given to Napoleon's wife and son by the Treaty of Fontainebleau, when Napoleon himself was granted Elba for his lifetime. The fate of Tuscany,

[1] The history of this tedious and obscure diplomacy has been illuminated by the work of Commandant M. H. Weil, *Joachim Murat, Roi de Naples, la Dernière Année de Règne*, 5 vols., Paris, 1910, which is based on an exhaustive study of the European archives. His conclusions are, however, open to objection on some points, and he has neglected to a certain extent the British papers.
[2] There is no truth in the contention, believed by many historians, that a secret treaty was signed at Prague in July 1813 between Great Britain and Austria regarding Italy.

Lucca, and a few other smaller principalities was, however, undecided. The Pope had been restored to Rome and the Papal State round it, but his Minister, Cardinal Consalvi, had in vain pressed at London and Paris for the restoration of the three Legations in the north of his territory, while Murat refused to give up the Marches of Ancona in the south.

Talleyrand from the first demanded the overthrow of Murat and the restoration of Ferdinand of Sicily in his place. To allow Napoleon's brother-in-law to remain on a throne was intolerable to Louis XVIII, but the policy was also Talleyrand's own. He wished by dynastic changes to increase French influence in Italy at the expense of Austria. In this demand he was vehemently supported by Labrador, who pressed also for the restoration of the Parma Duchies as well as Lucca to the Spanish Bourbons. This was also Talleyrand's object, but he knew its difficulties. He subordinated everything, therefore, to the overthrow of Murat, hoping to obtain some of his other aims in the resulting adjustment.

Murat had no friend amongst the Great Powers. Metternich realised as well as any how dangerous it was to allow a remnant of the Napoleonic régime to exist in Italy. England, the saviour of Sicily, whither she had conveyed both British armies and a British Constitution, saw in a Napoleonic Naples a danger to her control of the Mediterranean. The Tsar, while chivalrously anxious to protect the rights of the Empress and her son, had no inclination to protect Murat. Prussia had from the first given her opinion that Murat must go. Murat had to sustain, therefore, the active hostility of France, Spain, Sicily, and the Pope, without a single friend. His only safeguard was the treaty, and the rivalry between France and Austria. Two other forces might also work for him, but only at the cost of a war. The growing dislike of Austrian domination in Italy and the revival of hopes of liberty and independence, which had been implanted by Napoleon and encouraged at one time by the

Whig representatives of Great Britain, might rally all Italy to his side. There was also the Emperor at Elba. But, while these possibilities made it more dangerous to attack him, they provided also additional reasons why his throne should fall.

Metternich's plan at the Congress was to postpone the settlement of Italy until the last, and wait upon events. The incorporation of Genoa in Piedmont was, therefore, the only point finally settled in the first period of the Congress. Though Talleyrand objected, he could do nothing until the Polish-Saxon question enabled him to make the destruction of Murat a condition of his alliance. Both Castlereagh and Metternich had, as a matter of fact, long made up their mind that Murat must be abandoned to his enemies. The only question was the method and the time. Metternich had to break a treaty for which all Murat's mistakes gave no real excuse, while Castlereagh had to think of the Whigs who took an intense interest in Italy, and had already protested against Genoa's loss of independence. Both were agreed that French troops must not march through Italy; and to this condition Talleyrand was forced to agree. But Metternich wished to use the Neapolitan question to secure his other aims in Italy, and, Talleyrand proving obdurate, he had recourse to Paris. He had already in December been in direct correspondence with Blacas, who was jealous of Talleyrand. At the beginning of January, he sent through his Ambassador direct proposals to Blacas, of which step Castlereagh, who appears to have had his entire confidence, was fully informed. In these proposals the certainty of the ultimate fall of Murat was demonstrated, as well as the impossibility of Austria acting at the moment, or of allowing French troops to go through Italy. The advantages of direct correspondence with the Court of Versailles were also dwelt upon. This overture was well received at Paris, and Blacas was ready to act with Metternich to the exclusion of Talleyrand.

The finishing touches to this diplomacy were to be made by

Castlereagh, who, in spite of the remonstrances of Bentinck, had pledged himself to Metternich's policy. He had obtained the consent of Liverpool to the destruction of Murat in time for him to win Talleyrand's consent to all arrangements in Germany.[1] Castlereagh and Metternich determined that the final arrangements should, if possible, be made at Paris; and with this object in view Castlereagh, on his return, paid a special visit to Louis XVIII. He succeeded in inducing the King to go a long way towards granting the other Austrian arrangements in Italy in return for the promise that Murat should be overthrown; and new instructions were sent to Talleyrand, who was, however, ignorant of the game that was being played.[2]

This was the situation when the return of Napoleon broke up all these combinations. While it deprived Talleyrand of influence, it drove Murat into action. Though Metternich by skilful manœuvres had endeavoured to lull him into security, he could not help being aware of the danger of his position. He had probably had no share in Napoleon's return, which he regarded as a fresh danger to himself; but he thought that it gave him an opportunity to rally Italy round him while Europe was otherwise occupied. His troops marched to the north, and by the end of March he was virtually at war with Austria. England also declared war; and, as the Neapolitan Army failed entirely, Murat fled, and Ferdinand's restoration was accomplished. Metternich secured his main aims; for Ferdinand, who had been made into a constitutional monarch by England, was now pledged by a secret treaty to avoid any such experiment in Naples. Castlereagh defended his own conduct in the House of Commons by producing evidence, from documents supplied by the Bourbons, of Murat's so-called treachery; but even Wellington admitted that no case

---

[1] Bentinck to Castlereagh, Jan. 7, 1815, F.O. Continent 11; Castlereagh to Liverpool, Jan. 29, F.O. Continent 11.

[2] Weil, M. H., *Joachim Murat, Roi de Naples*, III, p. 12 ff. A copy of the document which Louis XVIII drew up is in F.O. Continent Archives 8.

K

was made out against him. The perfidy of the statesman was, however, hidden from Europe to a certain extent by Murat's own hasty conduct. This dubious incident is one of the greatest blots on Castlereagh's conduct, and it is made even blacker by the fact that he was at once made aware of the secret treaty with Ferdinand.[1] He could not indeed be held responsible for the extravagant promises which Bentinck and other Whigs had made to the Italians. His consent to the overthrow of Murat may be defended by the great necessity of securing a settlement at Vienna. But this does not excuse his active participation in Metternich's aims, which were not only to extend Austrian influence over the whole of Italy, but to stamp out the ideas of nationality and liberalism which threatened Austrian domination.

With Talleyrand impotent, the rest of Italy was partitioned to Metternich's liking. Piedmont, increased by Genoa and some accessions from France, was the only State which Metternich did not fully control; and even there he was aiming at changing the succession in Austrian interests. The Parma Duchies went to Marie Louise, the settlement of the reversion being left open;[2] Tuscany and Modena to an Austrian Archduke, while only Lucca was left to the Infanta Maria Luisa, the representative of the Parma Bourbons. The Pope regained the Legations of Ravenna, Bologna, and Ferrara, where, however, Austria kept the right of garrison. Austrian influence was thus perpetuated in the centre of the Peninsula. Spain refused to sign the Final Act because of the neglect of the claims of her house; and only later rearrangements won her assent in 1817. The

---

[1] A'Court to Castlereagh, July 15, 1815, F.O. Continent 11. The treaty was dated June 12, 1815. So early as September 24, 1814, Castlereagh had pressed for a modification of the Sicilian Constitution which should strengthen the power of the Crown.

[2] A secret protocol was signed at Vienna on May 31, 1814, at the instance of Alexander, without the knowledge of England and France, which would have preserved the rights of succession to the young Napoleon. It had, however, later to be disavowed, and the succession went to the Spanish claimant, the Duchess of Lucca, and her issue.

Ionian Isles, which had been originally designed by Castlereagh as compensation for Ferdinand of Sicily, were also affected by the changes in Italy. After Murat's fall, Austria would not consent to allow Naples and the Ionian Isles to be under the same sovereignty. The idea of handing them over to Austria herself was opposed by Russia, though England would readily have consented, and pressed this solution on the Congress. The matter was not settled until the second Peace of Paris, when a plan was accepted which had long been advocated by Capo d'Istria, to whom Alexander gave all his authority in this question; and the islands remained under British protection.[1]

Spain, whose interests had been handled in the worst possible manner, was also required by the Final Act to restore to Portugal Olivenza, which she had occupied in 1801, but this restitution, which was to be the cause of much trouble in succeeding years, was never carried out. For the rest, neither Spain nor Portugal received any recognition of their efforts in the struggle against Napoleon. The question of their colonial possessions was excluded from all consideration, no less by their own wishes than by the determination of Great Britain not to allow the Congress to discuss extra-European affairs, except in so far as they were connected with the slave trade.

Section 28. The Making of the German Confederation.[2]
The Swiss Constitution. General Questions

Though the Congress did not give Europe a Constitution, it at least laid down the principles of a Constitution for Germany,

---

[1] See Schiemann, *Geschichte Russlands*, I, 558.
[2] There is an enormous bibliography on this complicated subject. The documentary evidence is largely printed in Schmidt, W. A. *Geschichte der Deutschen Verfassungsfrage während der Befreiungskriege und des Wiener Kongreses.* The account by Sir Adolphus Ward, in the *Cambridge Modern History*, vol. IX, is the most impartial that exists, and is based on an unrivalled knowledge of the subject.

but the result of months of intense effort on the part of many sincere and able personalities was only to produce a Confederation which was a mere mockery of the hopes of German patriots. The truth was that there was not yet a sufficiently organised body of public opinion strong enough to overcome Prussian militarism, Habsburgism, and the selfishness of the smaller monarchs of Germany.

The factors of this intricate and obscure diplomacy reach back into the mediaeval history of Germany. Napoleon had substituted the Confederation of the Rhine for the worn-out shell of the Holy Roman Empire, which, in the hands of the Habsburgs, had been the only bond linking together the multitude of petty States, princes, and free cities which constituted Germany. The dissolution of the Confederation of the Rhine by Napoleon's defeat, and the reconquest of the territory which had been incorporated in France, raised the question as to what was now to be created in Germany. There was in Germany a strong feeling that German weakness before France had been due to disunion; and that some form of unity must be created to prevent a recurrence of past evils. There was also a strong democratic movement, somewhat academic in character, which hoped that this united Germany might be given representative institutions. The princes, however, had no intention either of sharing their sovereignty with their peoples, or of subordinating it to the common welfare of Germany; and their sovereignty had indeed been guaranteed in the treaties signed in the autumn of 1813, when they joined the Grand Alliance. Had Metternich, therefore, in 1813 or early 1814 consented to revive the shadowy suzerainty of the Holy Roman Empire in the Habsburg house, as he had been pressed to do from many quarters, there is no doubt that he would have had a large following. But he did not think it advisable to risk the opposition that would ensue from Prussia and the German patriots; and, though this idea was more than once revived in various shapes, it was never seriously pressed.

It was Stein, one of the creators of regenerated Prussia, who was foremost among the statesmen in pressing the schemes for a united Germany. He had the ear of Alexander, as well as a considerable following among German Liberals, and would have sacrificed Prussia's, or any separate interest, to the construction of a powerful central Constitution. By both Prussia and Austria, however, the interests of Germany were subordinated to their own advantage. Thus, when the question of a German Constitution came to be discussed between them early in 1814, it was directed mainly by the desire to secure their own position against one another and the other German States. The result was the adoption of the principle that Germany should be united by a Federal bond, which, as has been seen, was agreed to at Chaumont, and inserted in the Paris Treaties. Discussions as to the nature of this bond were carried on by Stein, Hardenberg, Münster, and Metternich throughout the whole of the summer of 1814; and by September a sketch of a Constitution had been drawn up, which would have revived the system of division into 'circles' which had at one time prevailed in the Holy Roman Empire. This scheme, which secured the lukewarm approval of Austria, was based on a plan drawn up by Stein. Though the position of the secondary States was recognised, the result would have been to place Austria and Prussia in dual control.

Had not the Polish-Saxon question hopelessly divided Austria and Prussia in the first months of the Congress, there might have resulted from this proposal a Federal Germany, united by many more legislative and economic ties than ever before; for a joint effort on the part of the two Great Powers might have overcome the opposition of the secondary States to surrendering any real portion of their sovereignty. But in the German Committee which, as has been seen, was set up to draft the scheme, though the two Powers adhered to their proposals, their rivalry in other matters, no less than the opposition of Bavaria and Württemberg, prevented any real progress towards the acceptance of the Constitution. Münster, in spite of his jealousy of Prussia,[1] and though he personally had many objections to the scheme proposed, supported a strong Germany, which was also greatly desired by the British Ministers.

The result of this disunion was to open the way for many other combinations. The petty States, having no means of securing representation on the Committee, united amongst themselves, and sent in a formal protest at their exclusion, while at the same time they declared for a single head to the Federation. In the circumstances this could only have been Austria; and, when the Committee suspended all operations towards the end of November, after repeated refusals of Württemberg and Baden to submit to the proposed scheme, Metternich seriously considered the revival of the Germanic Empire under the presidency of Austria to the exclusion of Prussia. Had a compromise not been found in the Polish-Saxon question, there can be little doubt that this scheme would have been used; and, as nearly all the smaller States were disgusted with the overbearing character of Prussian diplomacy, it might have stood a chance of acceptance. As it was, the period of rupture only produced from every conceivable quarter a host of ill-digested proposals, which revealed the outstanding fact that there was in Germany no real consensus of opinion on which a Constitution could be provided. Nor can it be said that the attempts to reconcile the conflicting interests of the two Great German States, the secondary Powers, the minor princes, and the peoples, showed any signs of political genius. The small body of really patriotic and liberal-minded persons, who desired a strong Germany, endowed with institutions capable of giving expression to

[1] Münster to the Prince Regent, Sept. 17, 1815, Hanover Archives.

ideas of self-government, had no influence among the diplomatists on whom the decisions really depended.

The scandal was, however, too great to be endured; and when, by the end of February, the main territorial difficulties were solved, Austria and Prussia agreed to take up the task once more. The German Committee was to be reconstituted on a much wider basis, and the proposals to be laid before it were to be of a less ambitious nature. But the Prussian projects, of which there always appeared to be an inexhaustible supply, were not approved by Metternich; and three months elapsed before the subject was in a sufficiently advanced state to be discussed officially. It was Wessenberg who produced a scheme sufficiently innocuous to be laid, on May 23, before a committee which consisted, besides Austria and Prussia, of Hanover, Saxony, Bavaria, Hesse-Darmstadt, and Baden, as well as delegates of the princes and free cities. Both the Netherlands (for Luxemburg) and Denmark (for Holstein) were also represented. In eleven sessions this Committee worked out, not a detailed Constitution, but merely the outline of a Confederation which it was intended to supplement at a later date. This was finally agreed to in the shape of Twenty Articles, which were signed on June 9, eleven of them being incorporated also in the Final Act itself.

A Federal Diet was to be the central organ of the thirty-eight States, of which Austria and Prussia were to be reckoned members for their German possessions only, while the Kings of the Netherlands and Denmark were included for Luxemburg and Holstein respectively. Austria had the presidency of this Diet, a position which, though it seemed merely a recognition of her ancient prestige, was of real importance, especially as, though the votes were unevenly distributed, the overwhelming preponderance of the two Great Powers was not expressed in the Constitution. Beyond recognising a common necessity to act together in war, and hinting at a Federal army, there was no common institution created except the Diet itself. Even the military union, which the measures at the moment in progress against Napoleon showed to be so urgently necessary, was not constructed. To the Diet was left the elaboration of the fundamental laws of the Confederation, including such principles as the liberty of the press; but Metternich, at a later date, was to use that central body simply as an organ of reaction. There was indeed in the Act no safeguard for the liberties of the people, except a clause that an Assembly of Estates would be set up in each country of the Confederation, and the insertion of a few fundamental rights, such as freedom of religion and permission to move from one State to another. The 'liberties' of the 'mediatised' Princes were treated with little more consideration, but they obtained many personal privileges to compensate them for their loss of sovereignty.

In these discussions the other Powers of Europe, though they took the Constitution of Germany under their protection in the Final Act, had scarcely any influence. In the earlier stages, it is true, Talleyrand had sought with some success to increase the dissensions in Germany. But both Great Britain and Russia were sincerely anxious for the construction of a united Germany, Alexander being predisposed by the influence of Stein to this view, which was, perhaps, against Russian national interests. His connections with Württemberg and other small States, at any rate, played no real part in increasing the difficulties of the situation. Castlereagh throughout used all his influence to promote union, which he regarded as a fundamental necessity for the equilibrium of Europe. The failure to produce anything better than the emasculated Constitution, which left a large part of Germany at the mercy of a host of petty sovereigns, was the result of many causes, but the responsibility must lie with the Germans themselves, and not with the other States. The rupture between Austria and Prussia over the Saxon question prevented a settlement such as Stein had planned, which, owing to their diverse interests, was, perhaps, in any case, impossible. The smaller States, already secured in their sovereignty by the treaties of 1813, made the most of this opportunity. The reduction of these States to thirty-eight was indeed a great advance, but this was mainly due to the French Revolution and to Napoleon, and not to the Congress. The institutions under which Germany had now to live were really quite inadequate to solve the problems raised by the Napoleonic upheaval, and contained the seeds of a generation of war and revolution.

The affairs of Switzerland, though complicated and full of intrigue, were settled without serious friction among the Great Powers, whose fundamental interests were not in conflict. A new Constitution was drawn up which modified the Act of Mediation of 1803, one of the most successful emanations of Napoleon's genius; and by the addition of Geneva, Valais, and Neuchâtel a Confederation of twenty-two cantons was formed. Stratford Canning and others held the balance between the more democratic schemes of Capo d'Istria, whose attitude was determined by La Harpe's influence on Alexander, and the reactionary views of Austria and France, who after some delay was allowed a representative on the Committee. The Constitution was ultimately accepted by the Swiss Diet, and was followed, as had been promised, on November 20, 1815, by the guarantee of the neutrality of Switzerland and the inviolability of its territory, which was also extended to parts of Savoy. This established a new principle in the public law of Europe, and may be considered as one of the most important results of the period, for the Great Powers had definitely recognised that their own interests, as well as those of all Europe, were best served by the exclusion of a small State from participation in future conflicts.

Of the three general questions brought before the Congress, that of the abolition of the slave trade was forced on the other

Powers by the vehemence of English public opinion, which acted as a never-ceasing spur to the English plenipotentiaries. As Castlereagh more than once complained, this insistence rather hindered than helped the cause, for the Continental Powers were convinced that it was due more to self-interest than to humanitarian motives. Castlereagh used every expedient to compel France, Spain, and Portugal to agree to an immediate abolition. Talleyrand gave him some support on the general principle, with a view to conciliating British public opinion, but refused immediate abolition, which was only granted by Louis XVIII after Napoleon had set the example on his return from Elba. Castlereagh succeeded, however, in obtaining a declaration condemning the practice of the slave trade, which was annexed to the Final Act, while, by a monetary equivalent, he induced Portugal to abolish the trade north of the Equator. Concessions in money and colonies were the chief expedients he used. But one suggestion of an economic character deserves special notice. It was proposed to exclude from the European markets the produce of those colonies which refused to abolish the trade; and, though this provision was never put into force, it served as a basis for a similar proposal made by Alexander in 1817 to put pressure on the revolted Spanish colonies. The use of the economic weapon in peace time for political purposes was, therefore, seriously contemplated by the Great Powers at this period.

The regulations for settling the precedence amongst the Powers and their diplomatic representatives showed a great advance on all previous discussions of this subject, and henceforward these formalities occasioned little inconvenience.

Part Four

THE COMPLETION OF THE CONGRESS

Section 29. The Return of Napoleon and the Second Peace of Paris

The position of Napoleon was one of the first points discussed at Vienna by the Ministers of the four Powers,[1] and they were all agreed on the danger of leaving him at Elba. All they could do, however, was to watch his activities as closely as possible by an elaborate system of espionage, and rely on British ships to prevent his escape. These precautions failed, and Napoleon was eagerly welcomed by a France that had already learnt to distrust and despise the Bourbons. The crisis at Vienna was already past, and the Powers were unanimous in desiring Napoleon's immediate overthrow. The eight Powers issued a declaration on March 13, which denounced him as a public enemy. The news of his success produced a renewal of the Treaty of Chaumont on March 25; and the huge forces of the Coalition were set in motion once more. But it was only with great difficulty that the military machine could again be organised. Austria was occupied in Italy, many British troops were still in America, Russia's forces had retired to Poland, and only in the Low Countries was there the nucleus of an army within striking distance of France. There were renewed the usual squabbles about the troops of the German contingents, the methods of subsistence, and the plan of campaign. Wellington brusquely refused Alexander's outrageous demand for his own nomination as Generalissimo, and a grand General Headquarters

[1] See Appendix IV, p. 160.

was again formed to direct the strategy of the armies which were to invade France from every side. Napoleon was thus given three months to organise an offensive, but the British-German and Prussian forces in the Netherlands sufficed to destroy it, and the imposing allied array was never brought into action.

During the Hundred Days it seemed as if the Bourbons had lost the throne of France. Alexander felt confirmed in his dislike and distrust of their methods; Metternich opened secret negotiations with Fouché, whose Jacobin intrigues Napoleon, posing as a constitutional monarch, had perforce to tolerate; Clancarty chivalrously defended Bourbon interests at Vienna; but the British Government added a declaration to the treaty of March 25 to the effect that the war was not being waged to impose a special dynasty on France; and Wellington, the strongest supporter of the Bourbons, in April regarded their cause as lost. A third declaration against Napoleon, drawn up in their interests, had to be abandoned owing to the differences of opinion among the Powers. A republic, the Duc d'Orleans as King, a regency, were suggested as expedients. Only as to the exclusion of Napoleon was there complete and irrevocable agreement.

The British Government, however, at heart wished well to Louis XVIII, and were secretly pressing his return on the other Powers; and, as Talleyrand had foreseen from the first, the new Coalition, of which Britain was the paymaster, immensely increased British influence on the Continent. The Waterloo campaign made Wellington and the Prussians masters of Paris at the critical moment; and as the latter cared for nothing but revenge, the former had the game in his hands. Fouché played the same part as Talleyrand had played in 1814; and this strange combination triumphed over the republican factions. Louis XVIII was brought back soon after the allied armies had entered Paris, to make once more terms with the conquerors of France; and, when the Sovereigns and the diplomatists arrived, they could do nothing but accept the situation.

The negotiations for the new treaty extended over four months. The allied troops, to the number of 900,000, poured into France, and lived there at the cost of the inhabitants. As they were at the same time earning subsidies from Great Britain, they showed no signs of wishing to leave. The brutal conduct of the Prussian and other German troops towards the French population was both militarily and morally indefensible, and merited the severe condemnation which the British Ministers hastened to express. Even these latter, however, pressed on the King a policy of severity towards Napoleon and his generals. In such an atmosphere a treaty was not easy to construct. Talleyrand, though entrusted with the negotiations, had not now the confidence of the King. Nor were the allies by any means united on the terms to be offered. From Prussia and the German States arose a loud cry for the dismemberment of France. The Prussian soldiers, intoxicated with their victory, demanded the final voice in their Cabinet; and Hardenberg confessed to Cathcart that 'he felt himself in the midst of Prætorian bands'. They were seconded by the Netherlands and the smaller German States, while Austria, afraid to oppose this national outcry, was vacillating. Huge indemnities, Alsace and Lorraine, French Flanders, Savoy, were considered as just spoil to be taken from a France which had brought upon herself this second defeat.

This insatiate rage was opposed by the Tsar and the British Ministers—the one from motives of generosity as well as policy, the latter, so they avowed, solely for reasons of State. Alexander hated the Bourbons, and bore a grudge against Talleyrand, but he was sincere in his assertions that he wished well to France. Castlereagh and Wellington, in insisting on a policy of moderation, were in opposition to the wishes of the Prince Regent, the Prime Minister, the Cabinet, and British public opinion. For two months there ensued a fierce struggle between the Allied Powers as to the terms to be offered to France; and Talleyrand had to look on, impotent to influence the decisions in the slightest degree. The Prussians came forward with large schemes for territorial changes on the north-eastern frontier. They wished to absorb large portions of Hanover, compensating the latter with Luxemburg, while the kingdom of the Netherlands was to receive large increases in French Flanders. Gagern, the Dutch Minister, was won over to this point of view, and did his best to persuade his King. At the same time Alsace and Lorraine were claimed by certain minor German Powers; and Austria, to some extent, supported them, looking to obtain compensation for herself elsewhere.

Castlereagh's first task was to convince his own Cabinet of the unwisdom of these schemes. In despatch after despatch he reiterated the dangers of tearing provinces from France. 'Security, and not revenge' must be the policy of the Allies. What was needed was to destroy the aggressive revolutionary spirit in France, and prevent the return of Napoleon. If this was assured, a strong France would be a beneficial factor in Europe, and useful as a counterweight against both Prussia and Russia. If the French were deprived of the conquests of Richelieu and Louis XIV, England would be committted to defend Europe against an irreconcilable and infuriated nation. Moreover, if once a policy of spoliation were begun, every Power would claim compensation, and another Congress would almost be necessary. The brutality of the Prussian soldiers produced an immense effect on Castlereagh, and modified the views which he had held at Vienna, while he had also detected a spirit of Jacobinism in their army.[1] In conjunction

---

[1] Castlereagh to Liverpool, Aug. 24, 1815, F.O. Continent 24; 'The influence in their councils is at present almost exclusively military. . . . You may rest assured that there is a temper in the Prussian Army little less alarming to the peace of Europe, and little less menacing to the authority of their own Sovereign, than what prevails in the Army of France.'

with Wellington, he did everything possible to put a stop to the system of pillage and systematic plundering, which they had from the first inaugurated in the occupied provinces; and he refused to listen to the wild schemes of dismemberment proposed. He succeeded at last in convincing his Cabinet. Having secured their assent, he pressed on the Powers his own schemes, which were meant, without inflicting permanent injury on France, to provide security for the future and reparation for the past. Security he proposed to obtain through temporary occupation by a European army of the northern fortresses of France, as well as by the dismantling of other French fortresses, and the cession of some frontier districts; reparation by the payment of an indemnity and the return of the works of art of which France had plundered Europe during the last twenty years, and which she had been allowed to keep by the first Peace of Paris.

Even these moderate proposals went further than Alexander desired, but it was not difficult to secure his consent. Metternich was at heart convinced of the truth of Castlereagh's views, and was easily satisfied as long as he could obtain some relief for the Austrian finances. The Prussians had, therefore, to give way; and these proposals were, with only small alterations, proposed to Talleyrand on September 20. He refused to accept them, but his position had already been made untenable by the Royalist reaction. Fouché had already been dismissed, and the King forced Talleyrand's resignation. He was succeeded by the Duc de Richelieu, an *émigré*, but a loyal and upright Frenchman, as well as a close friend of Alexander. He accepted the conditions, and secured, by the influence of the Tsar, some further modifications. Alexander, indeed, tried to claim all the credit for thwarting the Prussians; and the necessity for preventing him from obtaining too great an influence at Paris was urged by Castlereagh to his Cabinet as a reason for his own policy. But the real battle was fought by the British Ministers, for, if they had joined the

Prussians, there can be no doubt that the scheme of dismemberment would have been carried.

The final result was that France surrendered a small strip of frontier to the Netherlands; portions of territory to Prussia, which included the fortresses of Saarlouis and Landau; and a part of Savoy to Piedmont, besides demolishing the fortress of Huningen, which threatened Bâle. An indemnity of 700,000,000 francs, the payment of which was regulated by a special convention was levied on her, while she had also to agree to pay the claims of private creditors for injuries inflicted by the French armies. Part of this indemnity was to be used in erecting fortresses on her borders. An army of 150,000 men was to occupy the northern departments of France for five years, which might possibly be reduced to three. This army was placed under the command of the Duke of Wellington; and the ambassadors of the four Powers were to form a council of Ministers at Paris to regulate its relations with the French Government. Its expenses were estimated at 150,000,000 francs for each year of occupation.

There was thus a heavy financial burden. Efforts were indeed made by Prussia and the German States to make it overwhelming. The total of private claims submitted amounted to 1,200,000,000 francs, but Richelieu refused to consider such a sum. England and Russia supported him; and, after a long series of negotiations, the matter was settled in April 1818 for 240,000,000 francs. Some relief was also obtained by the fact that the army of occupation was reduced by 30,000 men in 1817 and removed altogether after the Conference of Aix-la-Chapelle in October 1818. Since Napoleon had left France without a debt, having made Europe pay for the wars he had waged, she was well able to bear the penalties thus inflicted on her, and found no difficulty in raising the money necessary from European financiers. The final result, was therefore to leave her still a strong and vigorous State, which had suffered less materially than any of the Continental Powers. But, though the statesmen at the time scarcely realised it, the balance of power in Europe had been permanently modified by the result of the Napoleonic régime. The male population of France had been seriously reduced in numbers. France had lost colonies, and, while all the other Great Powers had received large additions of territory, her own frontiers were substantially the same as in 1789. Even more important was the fact that the system of conquest pursued by Napoleon had been a complete failure, and only served to strengthen the enemies of France. Though there still existed an aggressive faction in the French nation, these results produced a permanent effect on the national spirit, which was to influence events in 1830, 1840, and even during the revival of the Empire under the third Napoleon.

Section 30. The Renewal of the Quadruple Alliance. The 'Holy Alliance'

In the opinion of all the four Powers, the peace of Europe needed some further safeguard than the treaties with France. This was to be found in a renewal of the Treaty of Chaumont, which had already been reaffirmed at Vienna. Castlereagh regretted that some guarantee had not been made against Napoleon's return at the first Peace of Paris; and his intention from the first was that treaties should now be signed which would 'make a European invasion the inevitable and immediate consequence of Bonaparte's succession or that of any of his race to power in France'.[1] He secured the approval of his Cabinet, and submitted the proposal to the Allied Powers. Alexander received the idea with alacrity, and ordered Capo d'Istria to draft a treaty. This draft met, however, with grave objections from Castlereagh. It would have pledged the allies to support the Bourbon dynasty on the throne of France,

[1] Castlereagh to Liverpool, July 17, 1815, F.O. Continent 21.

as well as the Constitution which Louis XVIII had again granted to his subjects, a policy which Castlereagh thought bad in itself; while no British Minister could sign a document which showed

'too strong and undisguised a complexion of interference on the part of the Allied Sovereigns in the internal affairs of France, without sufficiently connecting such interference with the policy which a due attention to the immediate security of their own dominions prescribed".

He prepared a draft himself in which his object was

'to keep the internal affairs of France in the background, and to make the colour of our political attitude and of our contingent interference as European as possible'.[1]

With a few small alterations, this draft was adopted. The treaty signed on November 20 consisted of seven Articles only, which affirmed the determination of the Powers to maintain the stipulations of the Treaty of Paris signed on the same day, and to exclude Napoleon or any of his family from the throne of France. It was this treaty that was the basis of the 'Alliance' of the Great Powers which now assumed the control of European affairs; and all the efforts of Metternich and Alexander in the following years to extend its scope were defeated by the tenacious opposition of Castlereagh and the open defiance of his successor. But, though confined to the specific case of guarding against the dangers of a Napoleonic régime in France, it marked definitely the ascendency of the Great Powers and the principle of the European Concert. Castlereagh throughout his career was an enthusiastic advocate of

[1] Castlereagh to Liverpool, Oct. 25, 1815, F.O. Continent 29, enclosing the Russian and English *projets*. Liverpool objected to the phrase 'souverain légitime' in Castlereagh's draft, and substituted 'Louis XVIII ou ses héritiers successeurs'. There is a note in his hand on the document; 'The right of the people to choose their King will become the subject of debate in Parliament if "le souverain légitime" remains in the treaty.' He insisted on the same deference to public opinion in the phraseology of the treaty with France.

the system of diplomacy by which the Ministers of the Great Powers met together at frequent intervals to discuss international affairs, and he was only too ready to incorporate the idea in the treaty. It was expressed in Article VI, which ran as follows:

'To facilitate and to secure the execution of the present treaty, and to consolidate the connections which at the present moment so closely unite the four Sovereigns for the happiness of the world, the High Contracting Parties have agreed to renew their meetings at fixed periods, either under the immediate auspices of the Sovereigns themselves or by their respective Ministers, for the purpose of consulting upon their common interests, and for the consideration of the measures which at each of these periods shall be considered the most salutary for the repose and prosperity of nations and for the maintainance of the peace of Europe.'

This was a real recognition of the advantages of a permanent Concert of the Great Powers. France was admitted to this Concert in 1818, when the union, and consequently the ascendency, of the Great Powers was at the highest point. But unfortunately the Continental Powers were to use these reunions to assert the rights of legitimacy against liberal and constitutional ideas; and the Concert, from which at one time much—and with reason—had been hoped was soon dissolved.

On September 26, 1815, the sovereigns of the three Eastern Powers had signed the Treaty of the Holy Alliance. This notorious and much misunderstood document was simply the expression of Alexander's mystical religious beliefs, which, under the influence of Madame de Krudener, had grown daily stronger during the campaign of 1815 and the stay at Paris, though, as has been stated, the idea was first suggested to him by Castlereagh's project of guarantee at Vienna. The document simply stated that the sovereigns would regulate their public acts according to the benign principles of the Christian religion. This 'piece of sublime mysticism and nonsense', as

Castlereagh called it, was meant to be signed by the Christian Sovereigns of Europe. The position of Great Britain was difficult—'what may be called a scrape', wrote Castlereagh—and it was eventually solved by the Prince Regent sending a personal letter which did not commit his Ministers. The Pope and the Sultan were also excluded from participating in the Christian fraternity. The Holy Alliance had no influence on affairs, except to produce in the minds of the peoples the suggestion that the sovereigns were leagued together against them. This suspicion was transferred to the real Treaty of Alliance signed on November 20, and in later years with truth. But the two instruments signed at Paris can in no way be considered as open to the reproaches which were later justly levelled at those who tried to use them for their own purposes. Both expressed in different form the longing for a period of peace after a generation of warfare. On this point there were few optimists among the statesmen; and scarcely one expected that the peace of Europe would long remain undisturbed.

Section 31. *General Observations*

The work of the Congress of Vienna was dealt with faithfully by the publicists of its own time, and has been severely handled by historians in the century that followed. The spectacle of a dozen statesmen transferring 'souls' by the 100,000 from one sovereign to another has inspired many mordant pens; and in the light of the history of the nineteenth century the validity of these criticisms cannot be disputed. Such criticisms, however, neglect the fact that the Congress was the close of one epoch as well as the beginning of another. The main object of the statesmen of the day was to overthrow the Napoleonic Empire completely; and in that object they succeeded to a much greater degree than they expected. The settlement of 1814-15 was governed by the expedients necessary to gain this end, which could not be ignored when the final decisions had to be made. Had any attempt been made to substitute for the contracts, written and unwritten, which had united Europe against Napoleon, the vague principles of nationality and democracy, so imperfectly understood alike by the peoples and the statesmen, the result would certainly have been disastrous. The primary need of Europe, once the Napoleonic tyranny was overthrown, was a period of peace; and this the statesmen at Vienna undoubtedly secured in a far greater degree than the most sanguine of the publicists of the time dared to hope.

The Congress was not without a principle; and it is not strange that this principle was derived from the eighteenth century rather than from the new forces that were springing into life. The moving spirit of any age is seldom judged accurately by the men of action who live in it; and it was not to be expected that the principles of nationality and democracy, which had inspired the first attacks of the Revolution and Napoleon, should be judged fairly by the statesmen who had the task of rescuing Europe from French domination. Nor were any of the dismembered nationalities, except Poland, yet ready to receive national institutions. The national spirit in Germany and Italy was there, in the sense of hatred of the foreigner, but not in the sense which made it possible for Germans and Italians to attain to national unity; the subject nationalities of Austria and Hungary had scarcely awakened to consciousness; and, if in the Balkans the Serbs and the Greeks were already alive, this area did not come within the competence of the Congress. To a generation, therefore, which had seen the dominance of a single Power, it is not strange that the principle of the Balance of Power should have appealed with great force. This, as has been seen, was the governing motive of Castlereagh's policy, which attempted to strengthen the centre of Europe against both the West and the East; and, as during his lifetime the West and the

East had almost entirely swallowed up the dismembered and demoralised centre, no other judgment could have been expected from him.

Talleyrand also endeavoured to bring forward 'legitimacy' as a governing principle; but, though Saxony (mutilated in the process) and Naples returned to their legitimate sovereigns, it cannot be said that this principle was followed with any consistency. On the contrary, a large number of the potentates, dispossessed by the French Revolution, never regained their sovereignty, and their protests at Vienna were unavailing. The Congress, in fact, found it necessary to accept the *faits accomplis* of the Napoleonic régime; and this meant the suppression of a number of small States, republics as well as monarchies—on the whole to the great good of Europe. In this way, though not consciously, much progress was made towards a united Germany, and a united Italy; though, paradoxically enough, these very changes were fiercely attacked by many of those most in sympathy with national aspirations.

More worthy of reprobation is the discouragement of the idea of self-government, which had already come to a fuller consciousness than that of nationality. Alexander alone, with some of his advisers, showed any sympathy with it; and it was he who secured the 'Charte' for the French with the assistance of Talleyrand, who was also aware of the fundamental importance of this aspect of the French Revolution. To almost all the other statesmen democracy meant nothing but anarchy and revolution; and among these must be included the Tory Ministers of Great Britain, who even secretly encouraged the attacks on the constitutions which had been set up with the direct connivance of British representatives. It was this policy that made the subsequent national movements take strange paths, instead of being an expression of the peoples' desires.

The failure of the Congress to give any adequate expression

to the nobler ideals of universal peace may also perhaps be condoned. As has been seen, the statesmen, once their dissension had been adjusted, did turn their attention to the possibilities of safeguarding the new Europe from aggression. But the return of Napoleon again made them direct their energies to preventing aggression from one quarter only. In inventing the 'Concert' they undoubtedly contributed in a very marked degree to the security of Europe, for it cannot be doubted that, in spite of all its failures, that system did much for the nineteenth century. For schemes of disarmament there was in Europe then no articulate demand. The French had still an inordinate pride in their army; Prussia had just passed a universal service law which evoked a willing response from the people; Great Britain was not prepared, in the slightest degree, to apply the principle of disarmament to sea-power, in which she had attained complete and overwhelming supremacy; the Tsar, though he initiated proposals on the subject in 1816, appears to have had no real intention of allowing them to affect his own vast armies; and in no country was there any attempt to coerce the Governments on this subject. Accusation on this score must, in fact, be levelled against the age as a whole and not against the statesmen.

These considerations mitigate the severity of the judgment that history must pass on the Congress. Yet it cannot be asserted that the statesmen concerned were equal to the opportunity presented to them. They were limited in outlook, too prone to compromise, lacking in faith and courage. None, except Alexander—and he only fitfully and irresolutely—made any attempt to do more than the obvious. They were content with expedients. They were men of their own generation; and, though they secured for Europe a breathing-space of peace, and in one or two minor points, such as the regulation of International Rivers, did much for the future government of Europe, they did little else to win the gratitude of posterity.

Appendices

APPENDIX I

DESPATCH OF VISCOUNT CASTLEREAGH TO THE EARL OF LIVERPOOL,
VIENNA, SEPTEMBER 24, 1814[1]

My letters of the 21st instant will have apprized your lordship of my arrival here. I found the Russian Minister, Count Nesselrode, and the Chancellor, Hardenberg, reached Vienna the day but one after. The Ministers of the Allied Powers have had four conferences, which have been principally occupied in discussing the form and course of our future proceedings. There has been but one opinion on the point, 'that the conduct of the business must practically rest with the leading Powers'; and with the exception of a doubt on the part of the Russian Minister, whether the Emperor may not press the introduction of the Swedish plenipotentiary, we are agreed that the effective Cabinet should not be carried beyond the six Powers of the first order, with an auxiliary Council of the five principal States of Germany for the special concerns of Germany. You will observe from the Protocol [A],[2] officially transmitted, as well as from that which I now inclose, that the Allied Powers have deemed it necessary to preserve the initiative in their own hands. I have concurred in thinking this line expedient; but, considering the complexion of the protocol prepared upon this subject (which is Prussian) to be rather repulsive against France, and a little more conclusive in its expressions than I quite liked, I thought it right to give my acquiescence to it with the qualification contained in the note annexed to it.[3]

The mode of assembling the Congress and conducting business next occupied our attention; and that you may see the succession

[1] F.O. Continent 7.
[2] Protocol of Sept. 22, 1814; D'Angeberg, 249; *British and Foreign State Papers*, II, p. 554.
[3] *Ibid.*, p. 555.

of ideas that have prevailed upon this subject, I inclose unofficially and confidentially for your perusal the memoranda which have been given in, rather as throwing out ideas than containing a formal opinion on the part of those who prepared them.[1] The idea that first occurred naturally was to constitute the Congress, and when constituted to propose to nominate a Committee to prepare a Projet of Arrangement for the consideration of Congress. But this course of proceeding was soon dismissed, as involving us without previous concert in all the preliminary questions of difficulty—namely, what Powers shall be admitted to sit and deliberate, and what only to petition and negotiate; what are to be the functions and attribution of the Congress; and by what mode they are to act and conclude. This led to another view of the question, which you will find in two papers of mine,[2] the object of which was to see whether, saving all questions in the first instance, we might not, through a preliminary meeting of plenipotentiaries, get the conduct of the business with a general acquiescence into the hands of the six Powers, with their auxiliary Council for German affairs.

The assembling of such a preliminary meeting of plenipotentiaries is certainly by no means free from objection. You will find this subject investigated in a further memorandum, prepared by Baron Humboldt, who assists Prince Hardenberg;[3] but the substitute he proposes has its awkwardness, as it too broadly and ostensibly assumes the right to do what may be generally acquiesced in, if not offensively announced, but which the secondary Powers may protest against, if recorded to their humiliation in the face of Europe.

The question remains open till the French and Spanish plenipotentiaries join us. Perhaps the most prudent course may be between the two propositions, and that the declaration of the six Powers should not contain any public avowal of what they mean in point of form to do; but that it should state reasons why the Congress should not be constituted till the plenipotentiaries, after their assembly at Vienna, have had full opportunity for confidential intercourse, and till there is a prospect that by such communications (without saying of what nature) some *projet* of general arrangement may be devised, more likely than anything that could now be hazarded, to meet the sentiments and provide for the interests of all concerned.

[1] See Appendices II and IV.   [2] See Appendix III.
[3] See Appendices V and VI.

I have endeavoured, as much as possible, to effect a coincidence of sentiment between the French and Allied Ministers, and I hope I have in a considerable degree succeeded; but, whatever may be their differences with each other, the three Continental Courts seem to feel equal jealousy of admitting France either to arbitrate between them or to assume any leading influence in the arrangements consequent upon the peace. . . .

APPENDIX II

MEMORANDUM UPON THE MEASURES TO BE ADOPTED PREPARATORY TO THE MEETING OF THE CONGRESS IN FORM FOR THE DESPATCH OF BUSINESS, VIENNA, SEPTEMBER 1814[1]

It appears clear, upon the first assembling of a body so numerous as the plenipotentiaries deputed to the Congress of Vienna, that no effectual progress can be made in business till some plan of European settlement can be prepared and ready to be submitted for their consideration, and, further, till the form to be given to the Congress, and the manner in which the business is to be conducted, shall have been previously considered and reported upon.

It is equally clear that such plan or report cannot at once originate advantageously with any individual plenipotentiary, unaided by the councils and suggestions of others, and that it can still less be expected to originate in the body at large. If so, it follows that a limited number of plenipotentiaries must be charged to prepare and bring forward the same.

The Powers most competent to frame for consideration a *projet* of European settlement, at once likely to meet the views and interests of the several States, are evidently those who have borne the principal share in the Councils and conduct of the war, and in the formation of the several treaties, which by the first secret article of the Treaty of Paris are recognised and declared to constitute the basis of the intended arrangement.

With this view it is proposed that the plenipotentiaries of Russia, Austria, France, Great Britain, Spain, and Prussia should charge

---

[1] F.O. Continent Archives 8. The English draft in Castlereagh's own handwriting, with pencilled corrections. There is a French translation in F.O. Continent 7.

themselves with this preparatory duty, and that until they shall be prepared to report upon the same the other plenipotentiaries deputed to Congress will, by temporary adjournments, suspend all further proceedings towards opening, in form, the said Congress.

That, in the aid of the above general Commission, a special Commission, composed of the plenipotentiaries of Austria, Prussia, Bavaria, Württemberg, and Hanover be appointed for the consideration of German affairs.

That to these Commissions should be referred all communications which may be addressed to Congress, and, in order the better to enable them to meet the general wishes, that the several plenipotentiaries not forming a part of the Commissions should be invited to a free and confidential communication of their sentiments to the same.

That the said Commissioners shall invite the other plenipotentiaries, as soon as their report is ready for discussion, to assemble and deliberate upon the same, first determining as to the form and mode in which the Congress shall constitute itself for despatch of business. In which consideration it will be requisite to decide what Powers shall be admitted to sit and deliberate in the Congress and what Powers shall only be permitted to appear before the Congress to seek restitution of territories of which they have been dispossessed during the war, or for the confirmation of titles to possessions [of] which, being acquired during the war, the sovereignty has not as yet been regularly ceded upon a peace by the lawful sovereigns.

It is conceived that no doubt can exist as to the indispensable necessity of a preliminary proceeding of this nature. The six Powers in Europe most considerable in population and weight have been suggested for the reasons above stated, as, upon the whole, the most competent to execute this duty.

Were the number of six to be materially extended the business of such a Commission must be proportionately retarded, and were *any* addition to be made a selection, in some measure invidious, would become necessary, unless an entire class of Powers of nearly equal dimensions should be included, to which there appears the strongest objection.

It is proposed that the above six Powers should be charged *ad interim* with arranging the police necessary for the Congress, and with the organisation of a bureau for the receipt and preservation of papers and for the giving copies of the same to the plenipotentiaries who may require them.

APPENDIX III

TWO *PROJETS* OF CASTLEREAGH ON THE METHOD OF OPENING
CONGRESS, VIENNA, SEPTEMBER 1814[1]

I

. . . A notice to be published in the *Court Gazette* of Vienna,
desiring the several plenipotentiaries now at Vienna to assemble
at the .... on the ....to
consider the measures proper to be adopted preparatory to the
formal opening of the said Congress for the despatch of business,
in conformity to the stipulations of the Treaty of Paris.[2]

A list of the persons presenting themselves for admission to the
said meeting, to be taken on their entrance, describing on the part
of what sovereign or State they allege to be charged with full
powers, and no person to be admitted who does not claim to be
so authorised.

When the meeting is assembled the Austrian Minister to announce to the persons there presenting themselves as plenipotentiaries the arrangements made by command of the Emperor
His Master for the accommodation of the intended Congress, the
local assigned for its sittings, the guard of honour and the officers
to be in attendance upon it, and that the emplacement so assigned
for the assembling of Congress would be considered by His Imperial
Majesty as possessing all the privileges, etc., attached to an ambas-
sadorial residence, with the police thereof subject to the direction
of the Congress itself.

The said Minister, or any other selected for that purpose, may
then call the attention of the meeting to the situation in which
they find themselves, and to the necessity of taking some measures
preparatory to the meeting of Congress, for the purpose of ascer-
taining with more precision than is set forth upon the face of the
article above referred to the nature and functions of the proposed
Congress, and also of bringing before the Congress when regularly
constituted the business on which they are called to deliberate, in

[1] F.O. Continent 7. The English draft is in F.O. Continent Archives No. 8.
Article XXXII of the treaty was to be quoted at the beginning of the
document.
[2] F.O. Continent 7 has; 'and also to secure the means of bringing before
them the business, etc.'

such a form as may best admit of deliberation and of a final decision.

He may state that this subject having occupied the attention of certain of the plenipotentiaries then present, a memorandum had been prepared for the consideration of the meetings, which he might then desire leave to read.

The memorandum in question, being previously approved by the six Powers, it would be for them to communicate it privately and confidentially to [such of[1]] the other plenipotentiaries now at Vienna [as they can confide in[2]], so as to secure their support of its contents at the intended meeting.

The proposition is so reasonable in itself as to render opposition from any quarter improbable; it must, at all events, be futile if the six Powers and their connections support it.

The advantage of this mode of proceeding is that you treat the plenipotentiaries as a body with early and becoming respect. You keep the power by concert and management in your own hands, but without openly assuming authority to their exclusion. You obtain a sort of sanction from them for what you are determined at all events to do, which they cannot well withhold and which cannot, in the mode it is taken, embarrass your march; and you entitle yourselves, without disrespect to them, to meet together for despatch of business for an indefinite time to their exclusion, having at the same time the option to confer with any of the plenipotentiaries separately upon the points in which they are more immediately interested.

The further advantage is that, as you meet informally in the first instance as plenipotentiaries and not as a Congress, nothing is prejudged and nothing admitted till the leading Powers have had full time to weigh all questions well and to understand each other. It is quite impossible this measure can meet with any serious opposition.

If such a temper should exist in any of the plenipotentiaries, it is better it should be compelled to show itself openly, in order that it may be met and suppressed at the outset.

II

Should the preliminary form of proceeding be approved, it remains to adjust the course of business to be observed in the Commission of Six.

[1] Not in F.O. Continent 7. [2] F.O. Continent Archives 8.

As the happy result of the Congress will depend on the spirit of justice, moderation, and accommodation which shall really subsist among the leading Powers towards each other, it is submitted that all definitions which seem at the outset to draw a distinction between them should be avoided. That the four Powers which have hitherto acted together should, upon the first meeting, endeavour to impress the two others with a conviction that they desire to act cordially and confidentially with them for the common interest, and anything marking a different sentiment can only be justified by some attempt on the part of the latter to disturb the course of policy on which the Allies were agreed, and which they still consider themselves as confederated to carry into execution.

That they should confer with the French and Spanish Ministers on the nature and division of the business, and the order in which it is most convenient that the questions should be taken for deliberation; and, as having been the parties to originate the several treaties which are recognised as the basis of the proposed arrangements, and to conduct down to the period of the peace the Councils growing out of them, the four Powers should declare their intention of bringing forward for the consideration of their colleagues such propositions on the questions in succession as appear to them best calculated to satisfy the spirit and provisions of their treaties.

This, without bearing the character of offence or distrust, will secure to them an initiative which neither France nor Spain can complain of. In order to put into form these several propositions, they must meet apart, and such meeting will afford them a facility for concert without appearing to act upon a principle of dictation. When they bring forward their propositions they will hear the arguments of their colleagues, and if a separate reconsideration is necessary it can always be secured by any individual member, without putting forward any offensive reason for the postponement. The good sense of the proceeding will establish its own purposes as we advance, the understanding being honestly to tranquillise Europe, and by every reasonable and becoming sacrifice to preserve the concert between the four Powers, which has hitherto saved Europe.

APPENDIX IV

BARON HUMBOLDT'S *PROJET* FOR THE REGULATIONS OF THE CONGRESS,
VIENNA, SEPTEMBER 1814[1]

On est convenu dans les conférences précédentes:
Que la multiplicité des objets rend nécessaire de les diviser, et de les traiter separément; Que le nombre des Cours qui prennent part au Congrès et la situation des choses exigent qu'un petit nombre dirige et surveille la négociation.

L'application de ces principes demande que la division des objets se fasse d'après un système fixe et géneral.

Qu'on éloigne toute idée d'un pourvoir usurpé ou arbitraire que l'exclusion de certaines Puissances de la direction de la négociation pourrait faîre naître, même dans la partie la plus impartiale du public; qu'on tâche, ce qui plus est (*sic*), de ménager l'amour-propre des Puissances et des Princes moins considérables.

Enfin, qu'on évite que des Puissances qu'on ne peut ni ne veut exclure de la direction générale de la négociation ne prennent par là une part directe à des affaires auxquelles, d'après la nature des choses, elles ne peuvent point intervenir d'une manière principale.

Il est indispensable après cela qu'à l'ouverture du Congrès même, on s'explique d'une manière franche et précise vis-à-vis des autres Puissances et à la face de l'Europe, dont les regards attentifs sont fixés sur une réunion aussi extraordinaire, sur la nature, le but et la forme du Congrès.

C'est de ces considérations que sont nées les idées suivantes, qui, en renfermant des propositions sur la forme à donner au Congrès, pourraient en même tems faire le fonds de la Déclaration qui doit précéder son ouverture, et qui pourraient y entrer, quoique seulement en partie et avec de certaines restrictions.

Le Congrès de Vienne n'est pas un Congrès de paix, car la paix est faite: il se distingue des Congrès de Münster et d'Osnabrück, de Ryswick, d'Utrecht, etc., non seulement par le plus grand nombre, ou la plus grande variété des objets, mais aussi par là, qu'il n'a

---

[1] F.O. Continent 7 and F.O. Continent Archives 8. The copies of a document of which the French is execrable have been rather carelessly made. There is also another Prussian memorandum which appears to be a shorter form of this one.

point du tout un but unique, fixe et déterminé. Le Congrès de Vienne n'est point une assemblée délibérante de l'Europe. Car l'Europe ne forme pas un ensemble constitutionnel, et, pour qu'il pût y avoir une pareille assemblée, la part que chaque Puissance devrait y prendre à la décision devrait être fixée, ce qui n'est, ni ne saurait être le cas. Qu'est-ce donc que le Congrès de Vienne? Ceci ne peut s'expliquer qu'historiquement. La Révolution française et le régime de Napoléon avaient changé presque toute la face politique de l'Europe. La guerre actuelle a mis fin à l'un et à l'autre, mais les différents rapports politiques des Puissances n'ont été fixés qu'en égard à la France, et que par le Traité de Paris. Il reste encore à compléter cette pacification générale, à remplacer par de nouvelles, les institutions que les évènements des dernières années ont renversées et déraciner quelques restes de l'Usurpation Napoléonienne qui menacent d'inquiéter l'Europe. Pour parvenir à ce but, on a appellé à un même endroit les Plénipotentiaires de tous les Princes et États qui, de part et d'autre, ont pris part à la guerre. On évite par là que les négociations particulières de Puissance à Puissance ne fassent pas naître des malentendus dangereux; on s'assure que les arrangemens qui résultent de ces négociations ne soyent point contraires à l'intérêt général et leur donne plus de force par la sanction, ou du moins la reconnaissance commune; on peut enfin convenir de certains arrangemens généraux contribuant à la tranquillité ou au bonheur de l'Europe. Par une pareille marche on supplée en quelque façon à l'institution d'une république Européenne à jamais et par elle-même impossible. Le Congrès de Vienne n'est donc pas *une* négociation seulement, pas même *un* ensemble de négociations étroitement liées par un même but, mais simplement un complexe de négociations différentes qui conduisent à autant de traités particuliers et qui n'ont d'autre rapport ensemble que l'intérêt général de l'Europe. La question Européenne se retrouve dans toutes, mais du reste elles se sont plus ou moins étrangères. Il résulte de là que toutes les Puissances qui y interviennent doivent s'abandonner mutuellement, avec la confiance commandée par la grandeur des circonstances, le soin de faire entre elles les arrangemens qui leur semblent convenables, et de délibérer librement et isolément sur ces objets, jusqu'à ce qu'elles viennent à s'accorder sur les mêmes principes, mais aussi prendre l'engagement de proposer ce dont elles sont convenues aux autres, de demander qu'elles le sanctionnent par leur accession aux traités, et d'écouter et de discuter les objections qu'elles pourraient leur opposer. D'où il suit de soi-même que chaque négociation peut être entamée isolément, que plusieurs peuvent marcher de front, mais que toutes doivent rentrer au centre pour y être munies de l'assentiment et de la reconnaissance de l'Europe entière rassemblée ici dans les personnes des différens Plénipotentiaires.

D'après ce qui vient de se dire ici, il est impossible de déterminer les objets qui peuvent se présenter à la discussion. Chaque Puissance et chaque jour peut en apporter de nouveaux.

On ne peut déterminer que le genre de ces objets, et c'est aussi le genre seulement qui influe sur la grande question qui doit être décidee ici:

Par quelles Puissances et dans quelle forme tel ou tel doit être traité?

Il y a trois de ces genres d'objets entièrement differens l'un de l'autre:

I

La distribution des Provinces qui par suite de la guerre et de la Paix de Paris sont devenues disponibles.

La discussion sur cette distribution et la conclusion des Traités qui la régleront appartiennent exclusivement aux Puissances coalisées contre la France, qui en ont fait la conquête. Ce sont leurs Plénipotentiaires seuls qui peuvent se réunir aux conferences sur cet objet. La France et les États neutres en restent exclus. Ceux à qui ces conquêtes ont premièrement rendu la vie y interviennent, non comme des juges qui décident, mais comme parties qui demandent à être écoutées et allèguent leurs titres.

En même tems la France a un double intérêt à la décision de cet objet.

Elle a le droit d'y juger la conformit avec le Traité de Paris et la question Européenne. Cette dernière question y intéresse tous les États neutres; dès que la négociation est parvenue jusqu'au moment de la conclusion, la France et ces États doivent par conséquent en recevoir connaissance et être écoutés, s'ils trouvent à y objecter.

Les Princes qui ont pris part a la guerre ne peuvent pas non plus être appellés tous simultanément à cette distribution; il y en aurait évidemment qu'on aurait également tort d'admettre et d'exclure sans distinction. Il faut donc séparer la distribution:

de la Pologne,
de l'Allemagne,
de l'Italie.

M

(1)

La distribution de la Pologne et la forme qui doit être donnée à la partie qui deviendra Russe sont du ressort de la Prusse, de l'Autriche et de la Russie, les seules Puissances qui peuvent signer comme Parties principales le traité qui la réglera. L'Angleterre y intervient pour la question Européenne, mais elle y intervient aussi d'abord puisque les trois autres Puissances sont interessées à se prévaloir de son intervention.

(2)

Quant à la distribution de l'Allemagne, il faut distinguer entre la discussion sur les bases et les principes qui doivent les diriger, et sur l'application de ces principes, et le détail qui en résulte.

Il faut considérer ensuite, qu'outre la question généralement Européenne, la distribution de l'Allemagne intéresse (*a*) les Princes de l'Allemagne sous le rapport de leurs forces respectives, et de leur organisation intérieure. (*b*) L'Angleterre, par l'importance qu'elle doit attacher à fortifier la Hollande, et à empêcher un agrandissement excessif de la France. La Russie, par l'expérience qu'elle a faite qu'elle peut être inquiétée jusques dans son sein, si l'Allemagne n'est point indépendante, sans parler des autres États limitrophes.

L'Autriche et la Prusse sont dans tous ces rapports à la fois et ont par conséquent éminemment le droit d'attendre qu'on ait égard à leurs propositions.

Or, la discussion sur les bases et les principes ne peut appartenir parmi les Puissances appellées en général à cette discussion qu'à celles qui peuvent se placer et se maintenir dans un point de vue Européen.

Ces Puissances sont la Prusse, l'Autriche, la Russie, et l'Angleterre.

Il fait en exclure:

La France, la Hollande, le Dannemarc, la Suisse, puisque, quoi-qu'ayant un grand intérêt à l'objet, ils n'ont, par différentes raisons, aucun droit d'y intervenir;

La Suède, puisque quoiqu'ayant sans contredit le droit d'inter-venir comme Puissance alliée et belligérante, elle n'y a plus aucun intérêt direct, ayant échangé la Pomeranie, et s'étant concentrée dans le Nord.

La Bavière et le Wurtemberg doivent intervenir à cette dis-cussion, puisqu'ils y ont et droit et intérêt, mais il ne faut les écouter que lorsqu'on sera déjà d'accord, puisqu'ils n'ont point de point central hors de la question et ne sauraient jamais la juger d'une mainère grande et impartiale.

Les questions qui se lient à cette discussion sont, pour en citer quelques exemples, celle de la Saxe, celle si la Rive gauche du Rhin doit appartenir exclusivement à de Grandes Puissances? Si la Belgique et même toute la Hollande doit faire partie intégrante de l'Allemagne? Si les Princes aggrandis par les Médiatisations doivent conserver toutes leurs acquisitions ou si l'on veut leur demander des sacrifices?

Les principes une fois fixés, l'application en détail doit appartenir aux Princes Allemands exclusivement, car une bonne constitution exige une certaine répartition des forces respectives, et la division des cercles demande de certains arrondissemens.

(3)

La distribution de l'Italie est etrangère aux Puissances du Nord, et à la Prusse.

Elle est du ressort de l'Autriche, de la Sicile, de l'Espagne, de l'Angleterre, comme Puissance maritime éminemment intéressée à la situation politique des côtes de la Méditerranée et ayant une possession importante dans cette mer.

Le Roi de Sardaigne et le Pape y interviennent, comme États formant des prétentions.

Le Roi de Naples est par la nature des choses exclu de toute part au Congrès, auquel ne peuvent être admis que des Souverains qu'on veut géneralement reconnaître.

Comme ces trois divisions de la distribution des provinces conquises sont, malgré leur séparation, pourtant, liées par des rapports généraux, il est à savoir s'il ne faudrait pas créer pour cette partie si importante de la négociation un comité dirigeant général, qui, sans entrer dans les négociations particulières, surveillerait et réglerait l'ensemble. Si l'on ne croyait pas trop compliquer la chose par là, la Russie, l'Angleterre, l'Autriche et la Prusse pourraient seules le former.

II

Second genre d'objets: Les arrangemens particuliers que quelques Puissances peuvent faire entr'elles, et qu'elles soumettent seulement aux autres pour être reconnus d'elles. Ces arrangemens peuvent être de différente nature et il est même impossible de les prévoir à présent.

Mais il y en a un infiniment important qui appartient à cette classe. L'organisation intérieure de l'Allemagne, où une nouvelle ligue doit remplacer l'Empire qui a disparu.

La discussion sur cette affaire intérieure et domestique appartient exclusivement aux Princes de l'Allemagne. Même la Russie et l'Angleterre ne voudront point intervenir à une affaire à laquelle elles ne peuvent prendre qu'un intérêt général, et où l'intérêt particulier qu'elles y prendraient naîtrait toujours seulement de considérations également particulières, et par conséquent étrangères au bien-être commun.

La Hollande, le Dannemarc, la Suisse pourraient y être appellés, la première pour s'unir en partie ou en entier à l'Allemagne; le second, y rattacher le Holstein; et la troisième puisqu'une alliance à perpétuité entre l'Allemagne et la Suisse serait on ne peut pas plus désirable.

III

Troisième et dernier genre d'objets, arrangemens communs pour le bien de l'Europe.

Les objets qui se rangent sous cette classe sont les suivans:

1. Les dissensions intérieures dans la Suisse. Les Puissances ne peuvent point permettre une guerre intestine dans le centre de l'Europe, et la confédération Helvétique elle-même demandera probablement la médiation des Grandes Puissances. Si elle s'adresse au Congrès, c'est-à-dire à toutes, ou si les Puissances sont forcées à se déclarer médiatrices sans sa demande, la discussion sur cet objet sera du ressort des Puissances à qui il appartient de délibérer sur cette classe d'objets en général.[1]

Si la confédération ne s'adresse qu'à quelques-unes des Puissances, le cas rentre dans la seconde classe des objets: c'est-à-dire des arrangemens particuliers faits de gré à gré. Mais aussi alors les résultats devront toujours être soumis à toutes les Puissances pour juger de la question Européenne.

2. Le Royaume de Naples actuel. Les Puissances ne peuvent souffrir qu'il continue à exister en Europe un Souverain que quelques-unes des plus considérables entr'elles se refusent à reconnaître; on ne saurait souffrir non plus que Naples et la Sicile restent dans une attitude continuellement hostile.

[1] Note by Humboldt; 'M. le Prince de Metternich a observé que d'après le Traité de Paris, la France n'a pas le droit d'intervenir dans les affaires de la Suisse, et je me range entièrement de son opinion.'

3. Le séjour de Napoléon à l'Ile d'Elbe, et les individus de sa famille. On ne peut plus nier que Napoléon et les individus de sa famille inquiètent l'Italie, la Suisse et la France. La Convention du 11 février[1] ne peut pas être un obstacle à lui assigner même, malgré lui, un autre sort. Car l'Angleterre et la France n'y ont accédé que pour certains points qui ne les lient pas envers Napoléon, et si l'on veut parler impartialement d'après les principes de la justice, les Puissances contractantes n'avaient aucunement le droit de placer au sein même des autres une cause et un prétexte de troubles. Quant aux individus de la famille, rien n'empêche de les faire aller où l'on voudra.

4. L'abolition de la traite des Nègres.

5. La navigation libre des grandes rivières sur laquelle la discussion a été expressément réservée dans le Traité de Paris.

6. Le rang entre les Ministres de différentes cours, objet dont il a déjà été parlé dans les Conférences de Paris.

La discussion sur les objets de cette classe appartient à toutes les Puissances sans exception.

C'est la question Européenne qui y est principalement, pour ne pas dire uniquement, agitée. Mais toutes les Puissances ne peuvent point délibérer, à la fois, ni avec une égalité parfaite; il faudrait donc abandonner la discussion sur ce point, et [laisser] la fixation des principes aux six Grandes Puissances, l'Angleterre, l'Autriche, l'Espangne, la France, la Prusse et la Russie, qui écouteraient après les autres, sur les principes qu'elles auraient posés.

Une réunion telle que le Congrès actuel, même avec la division la plus exacte de tous les objets, ne saurait travailler sans être dirigée; le cas se présentera d'ailleurs qu'on s'adressera au Congrès, et que le Congrès, comme tel, devra répondre à des demandes. Pour le pouvoir, il faut qu'il ne soit pas simplement un être idéal, pas seulement un complexe d'un grand nombre de Plénipotentiaires.

Il faut en conséquence au Congrès un *Comité dirigeant*, et ce Comité doit etre formé par les mêmes Puissances qui décident la question éminemment Européenne qui forme la troisième classe des objets de la négociation. Car le Congrès lui-même est une affaire Européenne et une des plus importantes. Ce Comité forme le centre du Congrès; le Congrès n'existe qu'en autant que ce Comité s'est constitué; il est terminé lorsqu'il se dissout. Toutes les négociations particulières et les traités qui en résultent doivent rentrer dans lui, et c'est lui qui doit les proposer à la discussion générale de toutes

[1] The Treaty of Fontainebleau of April 11, 1814, is meant.

les Puissances, et y soigner leur accession. Il doit encore avoir le droit de presser les négociations particulières pour ne pas laisser devenir le Congrès interminable.

Comme les négociations particulières doivent être soumises à l'accession et à la reconnoissance de toutes les Puissances Européenes, il faut encore déterminer:

Le nombre des États et des Princes qu'on veut admettre, comme siégeant dans le Congrès Européen;

Le mode de les consulter.

Il a déjà été observé que les États qu'on se refuse de reconnaître, et auprès desquels la continuation de l'existence est mise en doute, ne peuvent point entrer dans ce nombre. Ceux qui venant d'être rétablis, ne sont par là point encore reconnus généralement, sont dans le cas diamétralement opposé. Ils commencent, tandis que les autres finissent. Ils ont un intérêt manifeste à chaque question Européenne, et leur voix ne saurait être exclue.

En ayant égard au degré de forces et d'indépendance, on ne peut admettre aucun Prince de l'Allemagne qui n'a point des possessions hors de ce pays, à l'exception seulement de la Bavière (et du Wurtemberg). Les raisons de cette exception tombent sous les yeux; d'après ces principes il siégerait donc dans ce Congrès les seize États suivants: le Portugal, l'Espagne, la France, l'Angleterre, la Prusse, l'Autriche, la Bavière (le Wurtemberg), la Hollande, la Suisse, la Sardaigne, le Pape, la Sicile, le Dannemarc, la Suède, la Russie.

La marche très simple pour chaque objet en particulier serait la suivante:

Qu'il fût discuté jusqu'à rédaction approuvée et paraphée du Traité, entre et par les Puissances qu'il concerne directement;

Que le Traité fût porte aux Comité dirigeant, discuté et paraphé par lui;

Que ce Comité convoquât les Plénipotentiaires des États qui resteraient encore à consulter, et que le Traité fût aussi approuvé par eux.

La marche du Congrès lui-même serait:

De dresser et publier la déclaration sur sa forme;

De convoquer et de constituer le Comité dirigeant qui s'occuperait incessamment, et de ses fonctions comme tel, et des objets de la troisième classe.

D'établir les conférences sur les objets particuliers, et nommément:

1. Celles pour la distribution des Provinces conquises;
2. Celles sur l'organisation intérieure de l'Allemagne.

(Signé) HUMBOLDT.

APPENDIX V

PROPOSAL OF BARON HUMBOLDT TO PUBLISH A DECLARATION,
VIENNA, SEPTEMBER 1814[1]

La pièce approuvée dans la conférence d'hier[2] forme l'ouverture du Congrès pour les Grandes Puissances. Pour l'ouvrir également avec et vis-à-vis de tous les autres Princes et États, on peut adopter la mode d'une réunion de tous ceux qui prétendent être munis de plein-pouvoirs, ou celui d'une déclaration adressée par les six Puissances à tous les autres Gouvernemens et leurs Plénipotentiaires indistinctement.

Je proposerais de s'en tenir à ce dernier.

Le premier a l'inconvénient d'agiter dès le premier abord la question de l'admission ou de la non-admission de certaines Puissances. Car si l'on appuye fortement sur la circonstance, qu'on n'examine dans cette réunion les titres de personne, ceux qui ont mauvaise conscience sentiront ce que cela veut dire. Si l'on n'y appuye pas, ceux, qui voudraient exclure d'autres, comme la Sicile est disposée ainsi contre Naples, les Princes souverains de l'Allemagne contre les Princes médiatisés, deviendront inquiets et chercheront des éclaircissemens. Or, il est de l'intérêt des Puissances alliées d'éviter cette question jusqu'au moment où l'on pourra frapper efficacement ceux qui sont à exclure.

Une réunion où tout le monde est admis, où chacun retrouve son antagoniste et où tous sont congédiés sans apprendre bien précisément quand leur tour d'agir arrivera, trompera l'espoir qu'il vaut mieux de ne pas réveiller par une invitation personnelle.

La légitimité du Comité préparatoire enfin n'y gagnerait guères beaucoup.

Car on dirait toujours qu'il n'avait eu aucun moyen de s'opposer dans une Assemblée où ni le nombre des personnes admises, ni leur droit de votes, ni celui de ceux qui n'auraient pas pû paraître, rien enfin, n'est fixé.

Une pareille réunion ne saurait, selon moi, être bonne, que si elle

[1] F.O. Continent 7; F.O. Continent Archives 20.
[2] Apparently the Protocol of September 22.

avait le but d'examiner les pouvoirs et le droit de comparaître de chacun; mais c'est précisément ce qu'on ne veut pas.

Il ne faut point se dissimuler que le Congrès actuel est de nature à rendre également impossible d'inventer et de puiser dans l'expérience du passe une forme entièrement bonne et convenable.

Mais une déclaration imprimée au nom des six plus Grandes Puissances de l'Europe obrie au moins à plusieurs des inconvéniens d'une réunion personnelle.

Elle ne préjuge rien; elle rassure le grand public, qui, confiant plus volontiers les intérêts de l'Europe à 6 qu'à 16 Puissances, est tranquille de voir travailler les premières entr'elles; elle n'inquiète point les Plénipotentiaires, mais leur montre même que, selon les objêts, ils seront appelés successivement à plaider leur cause. C'est dans ce sens que la déclaration devrait être écrite. Le fonds en serait le contenu de la pièce d'hier,[1] les deux séries d'objets; les deux comités préparatoires; on ferait entrevoir que l'édifice de la reconstruction de l'Europe repondra aux plans conçus par les Grandes Puissances alliées dès le commencement de la guerre; on s'y arrêterait surtout sur le grand but du Congrès, le complètement de l'œuvre de la paix; la fixation de grands principes tendrait au bonheur général de l'Europe; on ne préciserait rien sur la marche des affaires en détail, mais, en parlant de la multiplicité des objets et de la nécessité de terminer bientôt, on ferait voir que chaque objet qui est de nature à le permettre, sera traité pour lui seul et entre les Gouvernemens qui y sont intéressés.

Cette déclaration devrait être écrite d'un style simple, et plutôt raisonné que déclaratoire, pour que, quelque soit l'issue du Congrès, on ne fût pas resté au-dessous de ce qu'ont aurait annoncé. Immédiatement après la publication, le travail serait commencé et presque tout le monde serait trop occupé pour glosser ou manœuvrer.

Les six Puissances entreraient en discussion sur des objets généraux, dont quelques-uns, comme l'abolition de la traite de Nègres, exigeraient d'y appeller d'autres Puissances pour être écoutés.

Les quatre en délibérant sur la distribution des territoires disponibles en Allemagne ne pourraient se dispenser d'y admettre dans l'occasion, la Hollande, la Bavière, le Wurtemberg et d'autres Princes Allemands, même le Danemark et la Suède. Le même cas existerait dans les discussions sur la Constitution de l'Allemagne. La Sardaigne et les autres cours d'Italie auraient enfin également bientôt leur tour.

[1] F.O. Continent Archives 8.

Quant à la légitimité du Comité préparatoire, mon opinion est la suivante: L'Europe ne forme qu'un ensemble idéal et la politique n'est point astreinte à des normes constitutionnelles. La seule mode, dont les Puissances Europeéennes peuvent agir en commun est en conséquence, que les plus grandes conviennent entr'elles, et se mettent en avant; que les autres y consentent tacitement; qu'on laisse la liberté à chacun parmi ces dernières d'énoncer son opinion contraire, et qu'on prenne même l'engagement de discuter cet avis avec elle. Or, c'est exactement ce qui se fait à présent par les six Puissances.

APPENDIX VI

PROJET OF BARON HUMBOLDT: MODE OF PUBLISHING THE DECLARATION OF THE OPENING OF CONGRESS[1]

Pour obvier au double inconvénient de faire signer la déclaration des six Puissances par tous leurs Plénipotentiaires, ou de la laisser sans signature, et par là sans toute marque d'authenticité, on pourrait adopter le mode suivant:

On dirait à la fin de la déclaration que, pour éviter qu'une déclaration qui n'avait pas pu être remise individuellement et qu'il avait fallu publier par la voye de l'impression ne soit point falsifiée, on avait résolu de n'émettre aucun exemplaire sans le faire vidimer auparavant par un des six Cabinets.

Chaque exemplaire porterait pour lors au bas la phrase: *Pour copie conforme* et la signature des Plénipotentiaires d'une des six Puissances.

On regarderait de cette manière la déclaration comme une pièce arrêtée et rédigée par tous les six Cabinets en commun, mais rendue publique par chacune des six en particulier. On se tirerait aussi par là de la question embarrassante: dans quel ordre on doit placer dans la déclaration même les six Puissances. Car il serait naturel que dans chaque exemplaire la Puissance dont les Plénipotentiaires en auraient attesté l'authenticité paraît à la tête des autres, puisque cet exemplaire serait regardé comme une pièce émise par son Cabinet. Il n'y aurait enfin, en adoptant ce mode, aucun inconvénient qu'un des six Cabinets communiquât, s'il le jugeait à propos, la déclaration à une puissance qui n'eût pas été reconnue par les autres.

[1] F.O. Continent 9.

APPENDIX VII

VISCOUNT CASTLEREAGH'S *PROJET* FOR THE FORMATION OF A COMMISSION TO VERIFY STATISTICAL CALCULATIONS

There appearing a great Discordance in the Statistical Calculations furnished by the different Cabinets, Lord Castlereagh suggests that the 5 Principal Powers who take the chief interest in the Territorial Arrangements on the side of Germany: viz., Austria, Prussia, Great Britain, France, and Russia, or, if it is thought better in the first instance, that the 4 Powers in execution of whose Treaties these arrangements are to be made, should each appoint a Person to verify conjointly these Calculations, and to settle by a common accord at what rate of Population the respective Possessions should be taken in the Distribution to be made.

It seems also of pressing importance to have a combined statement made of all the disposeable Territories and of all unsatisfied Claims upon them, distinguishing those Claims that rest upon the Faith of Treaties, etc., from those that rest upon Grounds of Conscience and Favor.

That this Commission should be especially required to report:

What the Nature of the Engagements are with respect to the reconstruction of Austria and Prussia.

What progress has been made in Execution of the same.

To what further Possessions that Power lays Claims.

What Territories can be conveniently assigned in satisfaction of the same.

That a Similar Report be made under their respective Treaties, compared with their actual State of Possession for Prussia, Hanover, Bavaria, Holland, and Wirtemberg.

That a further Report be made distinguishing how the other German Powers, whose Territorial Rights were by their Treaties at Frankfort less beneficially secured to them than was the Case with Bavaria and Wirtemberg, are likely to be affected by any arrangement which may be proposed in favor of the six Powers specially named.

APPENDIX VIII

MEMORANDUM ON THE TREATIES OF 1814 AND 1815 SUBMITTED BY
THE BRITISH PLENIPOTENTIARIES AT THE CONFERENCE OF AIX-LA-
CHAPELLE OCTOBER 1818[1]

The benign principles of the Alliance of September 26, 1815,[2] having been either formally or substantially adhered to by all Powers may be considered as constituting the European system in matter of political conscience.

It would however be derogatory to this solemn act of the Sovereigns to mix its discussion with the ordinary diplomatic obligations which bind State to State and which are alone to be looked for in the treaties which have been concluded in the accustomed form.

The present diplomatic position of Europe may be considered under two distinct heads: Firstly the treaties which may be said to bind its States collectively; secondly the treaties which are peculiar to particular States.

Under the first head may be enumerated the Treaty of Peace, signed at Paris, May 30, 1814; the Act of the Congress of Vienna, signed June 9, 1815; and the Treaty of Peace signed at Paris, November 20, 1815.

These transactions, to which all the States of Europe (with the exception of the Porte) are at this day either signing or acceding parties, may be considered as the Great Charte, by which the territorial system of Europe, unhinged by the events of war and revolution, has been again restored to order. The consent of all the European States, France included, has not only been given to this settlement, but their faith has been solemnly pledged to the strict observance of its arrangements.

These treaties contain some few regulations not strictly territorial, but it may be asserted that the general character of their provisions is of that nature, and that they contain in no case engagements which have been pushed beyond the immediate objects which are made matter of regulation in the treaties themselves.

It is further to be observed that none of these three treaties contain any express guarantee, general or special, by which their observance is to be enforced, save and except the temporary guarantee intended

[1] F.O. Continent 35.   [2] The 'Holy Alliance.'

to be assured by Article 5 of the Treaty of 1815, which regulates the army of occupation to be left in France.

There is no doubt that a breach of the covenant by any one State is an injury which all the other States may, if they shall think fit, either separately or collectively resent, but the treaties do not impose, by express stipulation, the doing so as matter of positive obligation.

So solemn a pact, on the faithful execution and observance of which all nations should feel the strongest interest, may be considered as under the protection of a moral guarantee of the highest nature; but those who framed these Acts did not probably see how the whole Confederacy could, without the utmost inconvenience, be made collectively to enforce the observance of these treaties, the execution of this duty seems to have been deliberately left to arise out of the circumstances of the time and of the case, and the offending State to be brought to reason by such of the injured States as might at the moment think fit to charge themselves with the task of defending their own rights thus invaded.

If this analysis of these treaties be correct, they cannot be said to form an alliance in the strict sense of the word. They no doubt form the general pact by which all is regulated, which at that moment was open in Europe to regulation; but they can hardly be stated to give any special or superior security to the parts of the European system thus regulated, as compared with those parts which were not affected by these negotiations, upon which, consequently, those transactions are wholly silent, and which rest for their title upon anterior treaties or public acts of equal and recognised authority.

Under the second head, viz., that of treaties which are peculiar to particular States, may be enumerated the Treaties of Alliance of Chaumont and Paris, as signed by the four Great Allied Powers. There was a Treaty of Alliance, deriving its principle from that of Chaumont, intermediately signed at Vienna, viz., on March 25, 1815, by nearly all the Powers; but as the stipulations of this treaty are declared to have been satisfied by the Treaty of Peace of November 1815, and to have thereby become extinct, it will make the statement more clear to omit the further mention of it in the present discussion.

The treaties anterior to that of Chaumont between the same Powers may be usefully referred to, as explaining the events which first gave birth to this combination between the four principal Powers of Europe, as opposed to France, at a moment when the great mass of those States, who afterwards joined the Allies and constituted with them the coalitions which, in the years 1814 and 1815, operated against France, were yet under the yoke of that Power.

The treaties of Quadruple Alliance concluded at Chaumont and Paris may be considered as treaties of alliance in the strictest and most enlarged sense of the word. They have a professed object; they define the steps to be taken in pursuit of that object, and they declare the stipulated force by which that object is to be attained and secured. These two treaties form one system, consistent in its purpose, but varying in its means.

The restoration and conservation of Europe against the power of France may be stated to be the avowed principle and object of both treaties.

The Treaty of Chaumont, in 1814, aimed at effectuating an improvement in the state of Europe as the preliminary condition to a peace with France, and at defending, by the force of the Alliance, the terms of that peace, if made. The Treaty of Paris, in 1815, had only to place the state of things, as established by the Treaties of Paris and Vienna, under the protection of the Quadruple Alliance.

The Treaty of Chaumont gave to this Alliance that character of permanence which the deep-rooted nature of the danger against which it was intended to provide appeared to require, viz., twenty years from March 1814, with an eventual continuance.

This character of permanence was additionally recognised by the language of the Paris Treaty,[1] the whole of the provisions of which proceed not only upon the admission of a danger still existing, but upon the necessity of keeping alive the precautionary arrangements of the treaty, even after the army of occupation shall have been withdrawn.

The Paris Treaty also aimed at specifying with precision, as far as possible, the *casus fœderis* upon which the contracting parties should be bound to furnish their stipulated succours.

Where that could not be done the object was to provide a mode by which the case in doubt might be decided at the time it should arise.

Three distinct cases are provided for in Articles 2 and 3 of the treaty. The two first, being cases of fact, are clear and specific; the third being a case of a mixed nature, dependent for its just solution upon the circumstances of the event which shall be alleged to give occasion to it, is left to be decided in concert by the Allied Courts when the moment shall arrive.

[1] Of November 20, 1815.

In construing the obligations of this treaty, the recital which its preamble contains is, no doubt, to be held in view. It serves to show the degree in which the order of things then established in France operated as a motive with the Allies in making the treaty, and the deep interest they felt in their consolidation as a means to the general tranquillity; but as it was not required that France should bind herself, in the enacting part of her treaty, to maintain inviolate the political order of things then existing, it does not appear competent for the Allies to consider an alteration in that order of things, whether legally effectuated or brought about by indirect means, as in itself constituting such an infraction of the peace as the Allies are entitled to take notice of, independent of the consideration of how far that change goes immediately to endanger their own repose and safety.

The principle of guaranteeing to both King and people the established order of things was much talked of at the time. By some it was contended that a species of guarantee having been given to the King by the arrangement for placing an army of occupation in France, coupled with the instructions to the Duke of Wellington for the employment of the troops whilst they should remain there, that the Allies should give the nation the same security for their liberties by guaranteeing the Charte; but neither alternative was adopted and no guarantee was given beyond what grew out of the circumstances above alluded to; a guarantee which was, in its nature, temporary, and was expressly limited to a period not exceeding five years by the provisions contained in Article 5 of the general treaty of peace.

The four Powers, it is true, took further measures of precaution in their Treaty of Alliance, signed the same day, as will appear by reference to the Fifth Article; but this article proceeds upon the principle that after the army of occupation should be withdrawn the Allies could only justify an interference in the affairs of a foreign state upon the ground of considering their own safety compromised, and that, independently of such a consideration, they could not justly claim any right of interference, or in prudence charge themselves with the task of redressing violations of the internal Constitution of France; in this sense the latter part of Article 3 is framed, being the only article in either treaty which touches the question. The true point, therefore, for consideration under this article must always be, Is the safety or interest of the Alliance so far compromised by the event as to justify recurrence to war; or is it a case, if not for actual war, at least for defensive precautions; or, finally, is it a case which, though more or less to be disapproved or regretted, neither justifies the former nor requires the latter alternative? The case admits in good sense, as well as according to the words of the treaty, of no other solution. It would have been impossible to have proposed to France an express article to preserve inviolate the order of things as therein established, for no state of things could be more humiliating than that of a State which should be bound to its neighbours to preserve unchanged its internal system, and that any fundamental change in it, without their consent first had been obtained, should in itself be a cause of war. If such a principle cannot be maintained for a moment in argument, the qualification of it, that the change to be tolerated must be legally made, is not less so; for how can foreign States safely be left to judge of what is legal in another State, or what degree of intrigue or violence shall give to the change the character which is to entitle them to interfere? The only safe principle is that of the law of nations; that no State has a right to endanger its neighbours by its internal proceedings, and that if it does, provided they exercise a sound discretion, their right of interference is clear. It is this right upon which the latter part of Article 3 expressly founds itself, and not upon any covenant supposed to be made by France.

The Allies are presumed to have a common interest in judging this question soundly when it arises, if they are of opinion that the circumstances of the case, prudentially considered, constitute the existence of the danger, against which the article intended to provide. Then they are bound to concur in furnishing the stipulated succours; but till the case arises none of the contracting parties are engaged for more, under this branch of the article, than an eventual concert and decision.

Having discussed and endeavoured to state with precision what the existing treaties have really done, there will remain open to fair discussion the question, Have they done enough, or does not much remain yet to be done? No question can be more proper for examination, and no Government more disposed to consider it, than that of Great Britain, whenever any clear and specific proposition shall be brought forward, always holding in view the inconvenience of agitating in time of peace questions that presuppose a state of war or disturbance.

The desire of the Prince Regent always is to act cordially with his Allies; but, in doing so, to stand quite clear in the view of his own engagements not to be supposed to have taken engagements beyond the text and import of the treaties signed.

The problem of an universal Alliance for the peace and happiness of the world has always been one of speculation and of hope, but it has never yet been reduced to practice, and if an opinion may be hazarded from its difficulty, it never can; but you may in practice approach towards it, and perhaps the design has never been so far realised as in the last four years. During that eventful period the Quadruple Alliance, formed upon principles altogether limited, has had, from the presence of the Sovereigns and the unparalleled unity of design with which their Cabinets have acted, the power of travelling so far out of the sphere of their immediate and primitive obligations, without, at the same time, transgressing any of the principles of the law of nations or failing in the delicacy which they owe to the rights of other States, as to form more extended alliances, such as that of March 25, 1815, at Vienna, to interpose their good offices for the settlement of differences subsisting between other States, to take the initiative in watching over the peace of Europe, and finally in securing the execution of its treaties in the mode most consonant to the convenience of all the parties.

The idea of an 'Alliance Solidaire,' by which each State shall be bound to support the state of succession, government, and possession within all other States from violence and attack, upon condition of receiving for itself a similar guarantee, must be understood as morally implying the previous establishment of such a system of general government as may secure and enforce upon all kings and nations an internal system of peace and justice. Till the mode of constructing such a system shall be devised the consequence is inadmissable, as nothing would be more immoral or more prejudicial to the character of government generally than the idea that their force was collectively to be prostituted to the support of established power without any consideration of the extent to which it was abused. Till, then, a system of administrating Europe by a general alliance of all its States can be reduced to some practical form, all notions of general and unqualified guarantee must be abandoned, and States must be left to rely for their security upon the justice and wisdom of their respective systems, aided by such support as other States may feel prepared to afford them, and as circumstances may point out and justify without out-stepping those principles which are to be found in the law of nations as long recognised and practised.

The beneficial effects which may be expected to be produced

by the four Allied Powers consulting together, and interposing from time to time their good offices, as they have hitherto done, for the preservation of peace and order, is considered as equally true with respect to five Powers, the introduction of France into such a system not rendering it too numerous for convenient concert, whilst it must add immensely to the moral weight and influence of such a mediating Power.

AUTHORITIES

TREATIES, PROTOCOLS, ETC.:

D'ANGEBERG, Comte. *Le Congrès de Vienne et les Traités de 1815*, 4 parts. Paris, 1864. With an introduction by J.-B. Capefigue.

British and Foreign State Papers, vol. I, 1812-1814: vol, II, 1814-15; vol. III, 1815-16. London, 1838-41.

KLÜBER, J. L. *Acten des Wiener Congresses*, 9 vols. Erlangen, 1817-35.

DIPLOMATIC CORRESPONDENCE, PRIVATE LETTERS, DIARIES, ETC.:

(1) *Austrian.*

GENTZ, F. VON. *Dépêches inédites aux Hospodars de Valachie*, vol. I. Paris, 1876.

KLINKOWSTRÖM, A. F. VON. *Oesterreichs Theilnahme an den Befreiungskriegen.* Vienna, 1887. Containing Gentz's letters.

METTERNICH-WINNEBURG, C. W. N. L., Prince. *Mémoires, Documents et Écrits divers*, vols. I and II. Paris, 1880. Also German and English editions.

(2) *British.*

CASTLEREAGH, Viscount. *Correspondence*, edited by his brother, vols. IX, X, XI. London, 1852.

JACKSON, Sir GEORGE. *Diaries and Letters*, edited by Lady Jackson, 2nd series, vol. II. London, 1873.

WELLINGTON, Field-Marshal the Duke of. *Despatches* edited by Col. Gurwood; vol. XII. London, 1847.

WELLINGTON, Field-Marshal the Duke of. *Supplementary Despatches, Correspondence, and Memoranda*, edited by his son; vols. VIII, IX, X, XI. London, 1860-64.

(3) *French.*

TALLEYRAND-PÉRIGORD, C. M. DE. *Mémoires*, vols. II and III. Paris, 1891.

TALLEYRAND-PÉRIGORD, C. M. DE. *Correspondence inédite pendant le Congrès de Vienne*, edited by G. Pallain. Paris, 1881.

JAUCOURT, Comte DE. *Correspondance avec le Prince de Talleyrand pendant le Congrès de Vienne.* Paris, 1905.

(4) *German.*

PERTZ, G. H., and DELBRÜCK, H. *Leben des Feldmarschalls N. von Gneisenau,* vols. III and IV. Berlin, 1864-81.

PERTZ, G. H. *Leben des Ministers Freiherr von Stein,* vols. IV, V, VI. Berlin, 1850-55.

(5) *Russian.*

MARTENS, F. DE. *Recueil des Traités et Conventions conclus par la Russie avec les Puissances étrangères,* vols. III, IV, VII, XI, XIV. St. Petersburg, 1875, etc.

MIKHAILOVITCH, Le Grand Duc NICOLAS. *L'Empereur Alexander* Ier, 2 vols. St. Petersburg, 1912.

Sbornik of the Imperial Russian Historical Society, vols. XXXI, CXII. St. Petersburg, 1880, 1904.

(6) *Miscellaneous.*

GAGERN, Freiherr H. C. E. VON. *Mein Antheil an der Politik,* 5 vols. Stuttgart, Tübingen, and Leipzig, 1823-45.

MÜNSTER, E. F. H., Count VON. *Political Sketches of the State of Europe, 1814-1867.* Edinburgh, 1868. Fuller than German edition. Leipzig, 1867.

FOURNIER, AUGUST. *Die Geheimpolizei auf dem Wiener Kongress.* Vienna and Leipzig, 1913.

WEIL, M. H. *Les Dessous du Congrès de Vienne.* 2 vols. Paris 1917.

HISTORIES, MONOGRAPHS, ETC.

BERNHARDI, T. VON. *Geschichte Russlands und der Europäischen Politik im XIXten Jahrhundert.* vol. I. Leipzig. 1863.

Cambridge Modern History, vol. IX. Cambridge, 1906.

DUVERGIER DE HAUVANNE, P. *Histoire du Gouvernement parlementaire en France, 1814-1848,* vol. II. Paris, 1857.

FOURNIER, A. *Der Congress von Châtillon.* Leipzig, Vienna, and Prague, 1900.

FOURNIER, A. *Historische Studien und Skizzen,* 2^e Reihe. Vienna and Leipzig, 1908.

FYFFE, C. A. *A History of Modern Europe,* vol.].London, 1880.

ONCKEN, W. *Das Zeitalter der Revolution, des Kaiserreichs und der Befreiungskriege,* vol. 2. Berlin, 1887.

ONCKEN, W. *Lord Castlereagh und die Ministerconferenz zu Langres am 29 Januar, 1814;* Raumer's Historisches Taschenbuch, VI, 3. Leipzig, 1884.

ONCKEN, W. *Die Krisis der letzten Friedensverhandlung mit Napoleon I*; Raumer's Historisches Taschenbuch, VI, 5. Leipzig, 1886.

PHILLIPS, W. ALISON. *The Confederation of Europe*. London, 1914.

RAIN, P. *L'Europe et la Restoration des Bourbons*. Paris, 1905.

SALISBURY, Marquess of. *Biographical Essays*. London, 1905. Contains an essay on Castlereagh published in the *Quarterly Review* in 1862.

SCHAUMANN, A. F. H. *Geschichte des 2er Pariser Friedens*. Göttingen, 1844.

SOREL, A. *L'Europe et la Révolution française*, vol. VIII, Paris, 1904.

SOREL, A. *Essais d'Histoire et de Critique*. Paris, 1883, 1894.

TREITSCHKE, H. VON. *History of Germany*. English edition, vols. I and II. London, 1915-16.

VIEL-CASTEL, Baron L. DE. *Lord Castlereagh et la Politique extérieure de l'Angleterre de 1812 à 1822*. Revue des Deux Mondes, June 1, 1854.

For fuller list, see the *Cambridge Modern History*, vol. IX.

ADDITIONAL AUTHORITIES

BERTIER DE SAUVIGNY, G. DE. *Metternich et son temps*. Paris, 1959. English translation by Peter Ryde, *Metternich and His Times*. London, 1962.

BERTIER DE SAUVIGNY, G. DE. *France and the European Alliance*. Nôtre Dame Indiana, 1958.

BICKLEY, F. *Report on the Manuscripts of Earl Bathurst*. Historical Manuscripts Commission. London, 1923.

COLENBRANDER, H. T. *Gedenkstukken der Algemein Geshiedenis van Niederland van 1795 tot 1840*, vols. VI and VII. The Hague, 1912-14.

DUPUIS, C. *Le Ministère de Talleyrand en 1814*, 2 vols. Paris, 1919-20.

FUGIER, A. *La Révolution française et l'Empire Napoléonien*. Paris, 1954.

GRIEWANK, K. *Der Wiener Kongress und die Neueordnung Europas*. Leipzig, 1942.

GULICK, E. V. *Europe's Classical Balance of Power*, London, 1956.

KISSINGER, H. *A World Restored: Metternich, Castlereagh and the Problems of Peace, 1815-22.* London, 1958.

MANN, G. *Secretary of Europe: the life of Friedrich Gentz.* New Haven, 1946.

NICOLSON, H. *The Congress of Vienna.* London, 1946.

RENIER, C. J. *Great Britain and the Netherlands, 1813-1815.* London and The Hague, 1930.

STRAKHOVSKY, L. I. *Alexander I.* London, 1949.

STRAUS, H. A. *The Attitude of the Congress of Vienna to Nationalism in Germany, Italy and Poland.* New York, 1950.

WARD, SIR A. *The Period of the Congresses,* vols. I and II. London, 1923.

WEBSTER, C. K. *British Diplomacy, 1813-1815.* London, 1921.

WEBSTER, C. K. and TEMPERLEY, H. W. V. *The Congress of Vienna, 1814-15, and the Conference of Paris, 1919.* Historical Association Leaflet. London, 1923.

WEBSTER, C. K. *The Foreign Policy of Castlereagh, 1813-1815.* London, 1931.

GENERAL OBSERVATIONS ON THE CONGRESS OF VIENNA AND THE APPLICABILITY OF ITS HISTORY TO THE PRESENT TIME
August 1918

TABLE OF CONTENTS

§ 1. Since the Congress of Vienna there have been many Congresses; but no subsequent assembly has had the task of creating a new Europe or been faced with problems of equal magnitude and complexity. Its history may therefore fairly be said to have assumed a new importance as the only precedent for a similar assembly to-day. The fact that this history will be almost certainly studied with a view to precedent by the Governments concerned adds to its importance, while it is even possible that its transactions may be specifically quoted in order to support the point of view of one Power or another. The differences between the period reviewed and the present day are indeed so great that they considerably reduce the value of these precedents. At the Congress of Vienna only European

Governments were represented, while the position that Great Britain then held is now possessed to a certain extent by the United States, whose interests, however, are not European in the sense that Great Britain's then were. The changes in the organisation as well as the ideals of nations; the alterations in the technique of diplomacy produced by new systems of communication; the awakening of public opinion and the demands for new international control, which far exceed in intensity any that were then called into being; the differences in the character of the enemy Governments, which do not depend so much as in 1814 on any particular individual—all these circumstances produce new problems, for which the Congress of Vienna gives little guidance. At the same time, the principles then revealed and the methods then employed are capable of some application to present conditions; and it may be that there is much truth in the words, written in July 1815, with which Gentz closed his severe criticism of the Congress:

> 'Si jamais les Grandes Puissances se réunissent de nouveau pour travailler à un système politique propre à consolider et à maintenir l'ordre public en Europe, à prévenir les bouleversements, que les guerres d'ambition et de conquête préparent aux nations, et à assurer les droits de chaque Etat par une sanction universelle et des mesures de protection générale—si jamais un pareil ouvrage s'accomplit, le Congrès de Vienne, considéré comme réunion préparatoire, n'aura pas été sans utilité.'

§ 2. Perhaps the process by which the Congress came into being and the diplomacy which preceded the actual assembly are as useful for this purpose as the history of the Congress itself. The construction of the Quadruple Alliance at Chaumont,[1] which, as has been seen, was meant to protect Europe in peace as well as in war, played a great part in subsequent events. It was designed, however, as a special safeguard against Napoleon and what he represented; and the accession of a peaceful Bourbon Government made it unnecessary, and temporarily produced new combinations. Yet its use as a weapon in reserve was also clearly demonstrated; and it successfully achieved its object, both at the time and in the period that followed. It enabled the Alliance to face the dangers of peace as well as those of war, and in this way produced a decided effect on the whole settlement. Its history is therefore worthy of consideration as an

---

[1] See page 50, section 8.

expedient suggested to Europe by the experience of an enormously powerful military despotism.

§ 3. No less instructive are the attempts of the different Powers to secure their own special interests in the Treaty of Peace before the Congress met. Only Great Britain was fully successful in this object, for, by the exclusion of all maritime and colonial questions (with the exception of the slave trade) from the subsequent discussions, and the recognition of the extension of Holland in the Netherlands, both by France and the Allies, she had secured her main ambitions in the Treaties of Paris. Austria, also, by securing Illyria and her Italian frontier, obtained much; but her interests in Germany and Poland were, like those of Prussia and Russia, left in dispute until the Congress met. The result was to leave Great Britain in a very favourable position at the Congress itself, and to make it possible for her to assume the rôle of mediator, which, on the whole she played with considerable success. It is obvious that such conditions must always be present in an alliance, however widespread the recognition that the general settlement is more important than any particular part of it. To obtain special consideration for its own interests, in preference to submitting them to the decision of an assembly, must always be one of the principal objects of every party to a combination; and this fact must inevitably play a great part in all discussions as to the methods of obtaining peace.

§ 4. The salient feature of the Congress itself was that it grew out of the circumstances of the time, and assumed a shape which was not designed by the statesmen who had summoned it. As has been seen, it was originally intended that the settlement of Europe should be arranged by the four Great Powers of the alliance amongst themselves and incorporated forthwith in the treaty of peace with the enemy. The Congress of Vienna would then have been—what it was originally intended to be—merely an assembly for the ratification and adjustment of previous decisions, in which both the enemy and the smaller Powers would have been allowed only to obtain concessions on minor points, on condition of accepting the arrangements already determined. The four Powers found, however, that their differences on fundamentals were so great that they risked their unity in the face of the enemy if a real effort was made to settle them. Nevertheless, even after the Treaty of Paris was signed, they intended that the main points should be decided among themselves before the Congress met; and it was the belief that this could be done that made them pay so little attention to the actual form which the Congress was to assume. The result was to enable their defeated enemy to play an unexpected part in the decisions of the Congress. The threat of his armed intervention was a considerable factor in the display of force by which they were ultimately settled; while the neglect to pay sufficient attention to the forms of the Congress to which the four Powers had committed themselves, without sufficiently weighing its possibilities, produced a very difficult situation when the assembly actually met.

The word 'Congress' has also been frequently used at the present time, but it may be doubted if the constitution and functions of such an assembly have been clearly defined in the minds of those who have referred to it. Since the military situation will be the main factor in determining these points, they can hardly be settled in all their details; but too much attention cannot be paid to the forms and organisation of such a Congress at as early a period as possible. The statesmen at Vienna more than once bitterly regretted that they had not been more successful in reaching a solution of such problems before peace was made; and to the lack of imagination and foresight which made them incapable of seeing the importance of previous preparation must be attributed much of the difficulty, delay, and danger of the Vienna Congress.

§ 5. First, as to the method of negotiation with the enemy. Apart from the abortive negotiations at Châtillon, which had no influence on the subsequent proceedings at Paris, there was no understanding with the enemy until his capital was taken, a new dynasty enthroned which could be trusted to sign a satisfactory peace, and a practical cessation of hostilities brought about. The first task was then to conclude an armistice, which resulted in the withdrawal of the armed forces of the Allies from France, though they remained in military occupation of all the disputed territory, the French troops withdrawing from the European fortresses which they still held. This was followed by treaties of peace between France and the principal belligerents, which it took a further six weeks to produce. By these treaties the enemy's frontiers were fixed and all colonial exchanges settled. But, owing to the want of agreement among the Allies, the future boundaries of Europe were left to the decision of a 'Congress', to which all the Powers which had taken a share in the war were summoned. The four Great Powers of the Alliance attempted to obtain control of this assembly by a secret article of the treaty defining the terms of peace, which

o

gave them a preponderating voice in the decisions. They had not, however, obtained the signature of the enemy to anything but a few points, while the position of the smaller Powers of the Alliance and the exact constitution of the Congress had been in no way settled. The four Powers made another effort to come to an agreement at London before the Congress itself met, but this too failed. So uncertain was the position that none of the Powers could disarm; and they had even to sign a special treaty by which troops were kept on a war footing until the final decision should be made.[1]

In order to avoid a position so dangerous, the first expedient must be the signature by the enemy of the outline of the terms of peace while the armies are still in being and the military situation is still the dominant factor. If it is possible to secure, as the British plenipotentiary endeavoured in vain to secure in 1814, an agreement among the Allies on the whole settlement, the enemy can be forced to sign this *in toto* if the military situation permits. Such terms need not be worked out in detail, but they should contain the outline of the whole settlement, and not merely one or two points, as was the case in 1814. They should also contain the functions and constitution of the subsequent Congress, which would then be an assembly for ratification, detail drafting, and adjustment. If these terms were sufficiently comprehensive in outline, demobilisation could then follow immediately—a course which would be likely to appeal to all the belligerents, in view both of the immense relief obtained by the reduction of the naval, military, and industrial forces now employed and of the fact that the Congress is likely to be of considerable duration. The terms of such demobilisation would indeed properly be part of the document on which the Congress would be based.

§ 6. If such a plan be successfully carried out, the forthcoming Congress will from the outset be of a very different character from the Congress of Vienna. The main outline of the settlement will already have been decided, and a definite programme for the Congress will have been drawn up. The precedents of the actual discussions at Vienna will therefore have less value. Nevertheless, some guidance in principle may perhaps still be obtained. The original idea of the four Powers was to negotiate with France on the European settlement only after they had settled the points in dispute amongst themselves. Their intention was to establish a committee of the four

[1] See page 65, section 13.

Great Allied Powers, which was to have the 'initiative', *i.e.* to draw up a plan for the reconstruction of Europe.[1] Only after this had been agreed to by the four Powers was France (with whom Spain was to be associated) to be informed of their proposals. The final decisions of these six Powers were to be referred to the Congress as a whole, i.e. to plenipotentiaries of all the Powers who had taken part in the war. Talleyrand, who was backed by all the small Powers, succeeded in defeating this plan. He did not, however, carry his own idea of appointing a preparatory committee, elected by the whole Congress, to draw up a preliminary scheme for submission to the whole body; and, as a matter of fact, for the first three months, the main affairs of the Congress were simply discussed informally by the four Powers. Only when these failed to come to an agreement was France admitted to their councils; and the territorial distribution was then settled by a committee of the five Powers, the constitutional questions of Switzerland and Germany being decided by special committees, and the more general questions by committees of the eight Powers who had signed the Peace of Paris.

The original intention of the four Powers was a sound one, in spite of the fact that their dissensions and lack of foresight prevented them from carrying it out; and it is capable of application at the present day, though, if the procedure recommended above be adopted, the main task of achieving union will already have been accomplished. The equivalent to the Committee of Four would then be an Inter-Allied Committee, which would determine the decisions of the Alliance and present them to the enemy. This Inter-Allied Committee can be sub-divided as convenience may dictate, provided (as is shown below) that there is proper provision made for harmonising its decisions. The enemy will possibly adopt a similar procedure; and, in that case, the final decisions will be made by negotiations between the two groups who have already come to an agreement amongst themselves.

§ 7. Such an organisation raises the question, which arose in such an acute form at the Congress of Vienna, of the position of the smaller Powers. Three of the smaller Powers had been signatories of the Paris treaties, but neither they nor the other smaller members of the Grand Alliance succeeded in obtaining more than a consultative voice in the decisions of the Congress. The protests made by Talleyrand were of no avail; and these Powers were entirely shut

---

[1] See page 79, section 15.

out from the Committee of Five which settled the main points. A small Power could only influence the main decisions through the agency of some Great Power which found it expedient to advocate its interests. This caused great discontent; and, while it was difficult to find any scheme by which the smaller Powers could play a legitimate part in the decisions, the utter disregard of their rights was one of the main reasons for the comparative failure of the Congress. The difficulty is not less today. There are a number of small Powers in the Alliance; and the exact relations between them and the Great Powers need definition. The dominance of the Great Powers, first established at Vienna, has indeed been strengthened and consolidated by the experience of the nineteenth century, but the legal position is the same today as it was then. Theoretically the smaller Powers have the same right to decide the settlement as the Great Powers of the Alliance. No one, however, believes that this in fact will be the case. But, while the ascendancy of the Great Powers is daily brought into evidence, their exact relations to their smaller allies is difficult to define, though on its solutions depends to a considerable degree the efficiency and smooth working of the Congress. It is essential, above all, that no opportunity be given to Germany to imitate the rôle of Talleyrand, and, by championing the rights of small nations, to create discontent and even open protest, which she can exploit for her own purposes.

§ 8. In endeavouring to harmonise the interests of the small Powers with those of the greater Allies, the cardinal point appears to be that the smaller are mainly interested on one portion only of the settlement, while the larger are virtually affected by the whole of it. It may be possible therefore to recognise the special interest of a small Power in some particular area, while recognising that there is a general interest which must in the long run override all local claims. It would appear that this can best be effected by dividing the Inter-Allied Committee into sub-committees, in each of which the small Powers are represented when their special interests are affected. It is probable, however, that agreement on some of these committees may be hard to obtain; and, further, the solutions of each particular problem are inter-related. While the smaller Power must consider almost exclusively its own interests in a particular area, the Great Power must survey the total result of the decisions over a wider field. In many cases it may only be able to give way in one quarter, provided that it receives compensation in another. In this general adjustment the small Power has not the same claim to be heard; yet machinery for its expression would appear to be a necessary part of the Congress arrangements. It might be created by the formation of an Inter-Allied Committee, composed solely of the Great Powers, whose function should be to receive the reports of the sub-committees to adjust disputes thereon, and to endeavour to find expedients to avert deadlocks which may well arise. This committee would be composed of the principal plenipotentiaries of the Alliance; its decision would in the last event have to overrule the decisions of the sub-committees; and its influence would be so great that it would be able to secure general acceptance of its decisions if these were made after the small Powers had had full opportunity of presenting their case. Such a body would give a unity and decision to the Alliance which it might otherwise lack. It would, in fact, do the work which was done at the Congress of Vienna by the Committee of Five, though only after the preparatory work had been done by the sub-committees on which the Powers, Great and Small, specially interested had been represented.

This committee might also act as the preliminary committee for such general questions as the creation of a League of Nations and the problems of disarmament. The initiative on these matters must come from the Great Powers. It is not likely that agreement on such subjects would be made easier by introducing the smaller Powers into the preliminary discussions. If the Great Powers can formulate schemes, these can subsequently be discussed with their smaller allies, and the whole then presented to the enemy Powers as the considered programme of the Alliance.

The essential point is that there should be a directing committee of the Inter-Allied plenipotentiaries so framed as to be capable of taking large views and reducing disputes on minor points, which often lead to embittered discussions, to their proper proportions. To obtain a satisfactory solution of the vast number of problems with which Europe is confronted, there must be a spirit of conciliation which it will not be easy to achieve. Though the theories of nationality and self-determination do not lend themselves, fortunately, to the same treatment as that of the Balance of Power, yet there are many borderlands in which compromise is necessary and indeed inevitable. For this purpose the work of adjustment, such as Castlereagh carried out in the Committee of Five,[1] will be as necessary today as it was then; and a body in some sense similar should prove to be the best organ for this indispensable work.

[1] See page 134, section 26.

§ 9. Even more difficult than the question of the smaller Powers is the problem of those States and Governments whose existence has not yet been generally recognised. At the Congress of Vienna one of the main difficulties of the early discussions was the position of such States as Saxony (which it was intended should cease to exist), or as Naples (whose Government had been changed during the war, and had only been recognised by some of the Powers). Talleyrand, by putting forward the doctrine of legitimacy, attempted to enforce principles which were meant to serve the interests of France; but this doctrine was never accepted and never universally applied. Many States, such as the petty principalities of Germany and the republics of Venice and Genoa, were absorbed in other States without their consent. The problem was indeed so difficult that it was shelved; and, as the Great Powers arrogated to themselves the right of deciding the whole settlement, a solution based on principle was never obtained.

The parallel problem of the present time is even more difficult; and, since the principle of the rights of small nationalities is universally conceded, it cannot be shelved in the same way as at Vienna. At Vienna also the problem of Governments was simply one of the legitimacy of a ruling house; that of States merely the absorption of a territorial area in a larger one. But today the subject nationalities of Austria-Hungary, Russia, and the Ottoman Empire have been liberated; and it is admitted on all sides that their former Governments can have no right to represent them. New States have thus come into being; and Governments have been set up which claim to represent them. In some cases the initiative has come from the Allies, but in others the Governments have been set up under the aegis of the enemy Powers. In almost all there is a dispute as to the legitimacy of the Government which claims to represent them. The difficulty of creating in these new States institutions in harmony with the principles on which the Allies claim to be acting was clearly demonstrated in the discussions at Brest-Litovsk; and the adequate representation at the Congress of such nationalities as Letts, Lithuanians, Ruthenians, Armenians, or Georgians is one that defies reduction to a principle; for, if these nationalities are to obtain the right of self-determination, they need institutions to express that right; yet these institutions postulate the existence of the State whose extent they are meant to determine.

In these circumstances the Congress of Vienna only furnishes the negative lesson of the danger of disposing of populations without securing their participation in the act. The question will have to be settled on grounds of expediency, as a contribution to which the following points may be suggested:

(1) The enemy should be required to cede all rights over these populations in the same way as did France in 1814.

(2) An Allied Committee of the Great Powers should be set up, to which experts on international law and political science should be attached, in order to adjudicate the claims of all representatives of such States and Governments to representation at the Congress, except so far as such claims have already been admitted by the Allied Powers.

(3) Arrangements should be made, so far as is possible, for the election of constituent assemblies, the frontiers of the States being provisionally drawn for this purpose without prejudice to future decisions.

It may be noted in this connection that the four Powers agreed by a protocol, signed in London on June 20, 1814,[1] that no act prejudicing the future should be taken in countries provisionally occupied by their troops, unless the fate of these territories had already been settled by treaty. This protocol might well serve as a precedent at the present time.

§ 10. A precedent of importance would also appear to be the Statistical Committee.[2] Though the statesmen at Vienna were only concerned with the numbers of population, and neglected almost entirely national and religious characteristics, they found great difficulty in making their statistics agree. The Statistical Committee was appointed to investigate and harmonise the figures produced by the several Powers, and it succeeded admirably in its work. It would appear probable that it will be necessary at the present time to establish figures as to nationality, concerning which great difficulties are likely to arise. If a special Statistical Committee were appointed on the model of that of Vienna, to produce as a basis for discussion agreed figures of nationality and religion, much tedious negotiation might be avoided. Such a Committee should indeed be constructed as soon as possible, so that the Allied Powers may approach towards an agreement on this subject before the Congress meets.

Such a Committee, in conjunction with the plan of sub-division under the direction of one general committee, would also conduce

---

[1] See page 105, section 21.   [2] See page 65, section 13.

to speed. It is important that the Congress should reach its decisions without undue delay. Though it may be hoped that demobilization will be rendered possible by the preliminary treaties of peace, yet much confusion and uncertainty will be occasioned by the fact that the state of many European territories must remain provisional until the final settlement by the Congress. Delay will not tend to produce a peaceful atmosphere, while it will prevent the return to normal conditions which is so urgently necessary. Protracted negotiations will also give an opportunity for manœuvres resembling those by which Talleyrand and others endeavoured to influence the decisions of the Vienna Congress.[1] An organisation, therefore, which will prevent friction on minor points and enable decisions to be arrived at speedily, is eminently necessary.

§ 11. Reference may also be made to the large part which strategical considerations played in the discussions at Vienna. The critical moments were largely influenced by the excessive demands of the Prussian and Austrian General Staffs; and these exercised at times an almost complete control over the decisions of their Governments. It was the function of Castlereagh, both at Vienna and later at Paris, to combat these pretensions.[2] For this work, though in Cathcart and Stewart he possessed two soldiers as assistants, he lacked an adequate military staff. Wellington could, of course, supply him with an authoritative opinion when he was present; but, in the early discussions at Vienna, Castlereagh had to rely to a considerable extent on the military opinions of his Allies. While it may be anticipated that strategical considerations will now play a less important part, the experience of the Vienna Congress shows the necessity of the British plenipotentiaries being adequately equipped to express an opinion on this aspect of the settlement.

§ 12. The form of the treaty was the subject of considerable discussion at the Congress of Vienna.[3] There can be no doubt of the wisdom of the decision eventually arrived at, in face of much opposition, by which all the separate treaties were combined in one instrument. When a large number of subjects have to be considered at one time, there is always a temptation to avoid the obvious difficulty of obtaining the consent of all to the whole settlement.

[1] See page 113, section 23.
[2] See page 134, section 26; page 155, section 29.
[3] See page 97, section 19.

But such expedients are likely to create more difficulties than they avoid. The decisions of the Congress will be the public law of the world: and each Power, in order to obtain the protection of all for its own special interests, should guarantee the whole settlement. It is essential, therefore, that the territorial settlement should be signed by every Power; and any reservations (such as were put forward by Sweden in 1815) should be regarded as hostile to the general interests. This will be still more the case if the treaty includes regulations for an International Government and disarmament, and economic conventions. It will probably be better to insist that a Power should not sign at all (as Spain in 1815) than to allow it to sign only parts of the settlement.

§ 13. Attention may also be directed to the elaborate system of espionage[1] instituted at the Congress by the Austrians, and the success of the British in defeating all attempts at the penetration of their own secrets. Similar precautions will no doubt be equally necessary today.

Finally, it may be noted that the period 1814-15 is marked by the birth of the Concert of Europe; and that the attention of publicists has constantly been directed to the schemes of the Quadruple and Quintuple Alliances and to the projects of guarantees[2] which were then brought forward. Such precedents are indeed of great value, but they need consideration in the light of the period immediately following the Congress of Vienna, when their true significance was revealed, and they are therefore excluded from comment here.

[1] See page 110, section 22.
[2] See page 102, section 20; page 161, section 30, and page 187, Appendix VIII.

INDEX